Praise for *On the Edge: An Odyssey*

"I thought my life was interesting until I read Steve Murphy's *On the Edge*. Now I feel like I've been sitting in a rocker on the front porch."

—Steven Bavaria, author, *Too Greedy for Adam Smith*; former international banker

"Stephen Murphy has indeed taken paths less travelled. This is a frank and personal discussion of success, failure, and lessons learned by a Seattle boy who became a global wanderer."

—Christopher T. Bayley, author, *Seattle Justice*; chair, Stewardship Partners; and former King County prosecuting attorney

"Intriguing and passionate! Stephen's remarkable journey from the University of Washington to Harvard and Columbia Business Schools, Vietnam, Brazil—even Washington, DC—proves fascinating reading. That his fraternity created many friendships provides endorsement to true brotherhood today."

—James D. Boyle, president, Phi Kappa Psi Fraternity, UW, 1993

"*On the Edge* seeks to recollect the author's life with large strokes, while zooming in on specific events that stand out. However, it is not a story told without purpose. Rather, the author's life story is shown to be one of seeking his raison d'être…finally coming to find meaning in faith and in connecting peoples of the Americas. This book was a great read, and I am thankful that you have decided to share your adventures and lessons learned with many readers."

—Jon, editor, CreateSpace

"Esteban has led an intense and passionate life, hitchhiking throughout Mexico and living in Rio's hills—full of intrigue! His story provides inspiration to young professionals to 'land on their feet,' like we did in recent adventures in Havana."

—Professor José Antonio Echenique, former dean of Finance, Universidad Nacional Autónoma de México

"As a mother of three children, I want them to be open to what life brings, sometimes stepping off the path. Steve's memoir illustrates the point, suggesting hope to those willing to act on what life offers up."
—Julianne Casey Forgo, information developer, IBM Collaboration Solutions, Littleton, Massachusetts

"While chronicling life through twists and turns, this story is for all people unafraid to admit mistakes. Well done and uplifting, it often reads like fiction."
—Dennis Gibb, author, *Exordium: a Story of Everything*, and president, Sweetwater Investments, Redmond, Washington

"Steve's early days in Rio de Janeiro—living in a favela and hanging out with street kids—are unusual for a staid banker. Though sometimes iconoclastic, his words and actions always give hope."
—William F. Hamilton, director, BankBoston (BKB) Alumni, and vice president, UBS Financial Services, Boston

"Steve is incredibly curious about the human condition and open to new ways of thinking about how we can play better in the world sandbox."
—Robert Mahoney, president and CEO, Belmont Savings Bank, and former colleague, BKB and Columbia Business School

"This book is a must read for anyone from the turbulent sixties to the improbable teens of the twenty-first century, written by a man with clear and open eyes."
—John M. Meyer, past president, University of Washington Alumni Association, and retired Superior Court judge

"Steve has an incredible and enduring curiosity about humanity and our world. This is a story of a life well and fully lived!"
—Joseph M. Phillips Jr., dean, Albers School of Business and Economics, Seattle University

"*On the Edge* delivers much passion and adventure, delighting readers with Hollywood stories, including those from sometimes chaotic Brazil."
  --Marcos Rosset, former president, the Walt Disney Company (Brazil).

"The author's inquisitiveness concerning the human soul enables him to understand and describe Brazilians of all walks of life, as retold in *On the Edge: An Odyssey*."
  —Johnny Saad, CEO, Bandeirantes Communication Group of Brazil

"Steve battled video pirates and survived. His high-octane adventures provide fast reading for those keen on showbiz south of the border."
  —Steve Solot, author, *Brazil Cinema Today*; president, Rio de
  Janeiro Film Commission; and former senior vice president,
  Motion Picture Association in Latin America

"Meaningful to me is his life story—a circuitous route 'on the edge.' As a person of faith, I see, in his life, the familiar path of so many everyday saints."
  —Fr. Todd O. Strange, pastor, St. Joseph's Catholic Church
  and School, Issaquah, Washington

"Few people capture the spirit of service better than Stephen in his remarkable *On the Edge*. His search for purpose takes the form of a true odyssey. His generosity of spirit created the Pixote Literacy Fund, modeling how a professional person can have a meaningful impact on children."
  —Steve Vetter, author, *Soul Deep*, and chairman and CEO,
  Partners of the Americas, Washington, DC

On The Edge

On The Edge

AN ODYSSEY

Stephen E. Murphy

Odyssey Chapters

Seattle, Washington

ISBN: **1536851876**
ISBN 13: **9781536851878**
Library of Congress Control Number: **2016914336**

Odyssey Chapters, Seattle, Washington.

We'd love to hear from you via email: ontheedgeanodyssey@gmail.com

For the anonymous priest

Contents

On The Edge

AN ODYSSEY

Prologue

I CLIMBED UP many steps, feeling a stiff breeze. At the first deck, I stopped to quickly observe across the large lake. Onward I climbed, finally reaching the top of the tower—the breeze stronger at thirty-five feet. I went to the edge, looked over briefly, pulled back, but then jumped in.

Sometimes, I'd do the cannon ball. Other times, I'd hold my nose, counting the seconds while falling down. Before hitting water, I had second thoughts. But once taking the plunge, gravity pulled me down. Though a mediocre diver, occasionally I'd show off like Acapulco's best, crashing into Lake Washington with belly flops. Yet my body was supple and my spirit daring. I was "youth eternal" and could push life to its limits. Or so I thought.

On the day of those letters, I returned to the beach club, where my mother hosted picnics. That spring day, I went solo, climbing up those steps. I looked over again: Was I prepared to take a greater leap, this time "to the other side"?

Dripping, I walked home and found my parents reviewing school letters. I'd applied to three MBA programs: two had accepted me—Harvard and Columbia Business Schools. Stanford had not. Mom brimmed with happiness; their eldest and recent University of Washington (UW) graduate was accepted to the Ivy League.

At the UW, I lived at home, though sometimes at the fraternity, to keep expenses in check. Ivy tuition was thirty times dearer—I'd use up all savings in just one semester. Still, I pushed the envelope with my finances, little knowing that step was a new beginning.

I'd leave the nest and safety of my hometown. I'd venture east in a journey into a vast unknown.

But first, I had to choose between two fine schools. I chose Harvard of course; John F. Kennedy, my hero, went there. Though he attended Harvard College, not Harvard Business School (HBS), he still "parked the car in Harvard yard."

JFK held emotional appeal, inspiring me—of the sixties generation— to step out. Active in student politics and in Governor Dan's campaign, I dreamt big. Maybe I could follow his footsteps from the Ivies to elected office.

Taking a deep breath, I sent in my acceptance. I thanked Governor Dan and my sponsors, who'd written on my behalf. As a heady senior, I composed a mini-memoir about my thinking and actions, naming it, *"Je Pense, Donc Je Suis,"* after René Descartes's famous sentence, "I think, therefore I am."

Descartes's words became my mantra. By thinking and acting on a personal goal—despite risk of failure—I could attain student body office or attend the Ivy League. Through eighty-eight pages, I reviewed undergrad life, as a student activist and politico, advocating the power of positive thinking. Completed while packing my bags to Harvard, I sent copies to friends, family, and my UW heroes, Professors Costigan and Buechel. Today, only UW's library retains an original copy in the Allen Library stacks—the other copies having gone to the wind.

On the Edge: An Odyssey thus serves as bookend, recounting my journey, often at risk. I've highlighted *turning points* in italics, while stepping out to exotic places and situations. Those wanting to live or work abroad—especially in Brazil or Latin America—may appreciate my odyssey through twists and turns. You may ask about hazards of living abroad or returning home to reverse culture shock. Perhaps you'll wonder, as have I, if an "invisible hand" guided me through strong currents of life. Maybe you'll inquire, as Odysseus did, if destiny had the last laugh.

Through twelve chapters, I retell this story, beginning with my leap to the East Coast and the momentous challenges at HBS.

For young professionals mapping out future life paths, this memoir may prove frustrating. For those venturing on paths less travelled, it may lend confidence to land on your feet. Despite hard circumstances in family and school or corporate intrigue, I assure you that life exists beyond tragedy and disappointment.

Shall we dive in?

CHAPTER 1

Harvard Business School

HARVARD IS QUINTESSENTIALLY Ivy League. Its college was founded in 1636 and the School of Business and Public Administration in 1908, initially to school diplomats in business and public service. Harvard offered a master of business administration (MBA), and corporate America took note. Soon, Harvard MBAs became hallmark in business boardrooms around the world.

In late August of 1966, I looked up at Baker Library and saw ivy clinging to its sides—it really was there! The sun reflected off the library's cupola, and Harvard's crew rowed up the Charles River, sweating under broiling sun. Wiping my brow, I didn't mind the heat but pinched myself again to say, "I'm really in the Ivy League."

"Good luck, son. Send us news," my parents bid as I boarded my first transcontinental flight. With butterflies in my stomach, I'd set my face toward the east. I'd be the only graduating UW student to enter Harvard Business School that year.

I stumbled upstairs to the dorm with a big suitcase and ran into Frank. Of Italian American heritage, he'd graduated from Princeton, with a sharp sense of humor and intellect. "How's the land of cowboys and Indians?" he inquired.

"Still chilling out," I replied and remembered why we'd been paired—to encourage us Catholics to attend Mass. Though his father was a corporate executive from Jersey and mine a small businessman from Seattle, we'd connected through common faith.

That weekend, I joined classmates heading to New York. My first time in the Big Apple, I tried not to gawk. Feeling underdressed on Fifth Avenue, I suggested a change of venue to reluctant classmates. With few blacks in Seattle, I was curious about Harlem, and there we went. I felt self-conscious on Lennox at W. 125th but kept walking, looking right and left.

"Look what you've got us into, Murphy," grumbled a student from the Midwest.

"Think of this as an educational experience," I replied, nodding at black teens shooting hoops.

We aimed toward Morningside Heights and the setting sun and climbed the stairs briskly to Columbia's safe grounds. Its campus had an urban tinge, compared to posh HBS. Celebrating our Harlem experience, we wolfed down Cuban sandwiches and *cervezas* off Broadway, feeling good.

Back at HBS, I brushed lint off my coat, tied a Windsor, and got ready for the first day of class. I entered Section C into a mini-coliseum, spiraling up from where the professor conducted class. I sat toward the back as Frank greeted former classmates. Students congregated by Ivy schools, with me solo from the Pacific Northwest.

HBS students averaged twenty-six years compared to Frank's and my twenty-two. I counted three women and few internationals in our section of one hundred. We wore coat and tie—save one student from Mississippi—to emulate how young executives would look and act. Older students enjoyed this role, but for me, it was a challenging academic and cultural milieu.

Harvard, renowned for case discussions, charged us to review corporate histories, gleaning principles through discussion and inference. Even quantitative courses like statistics were taught that way. Classmates with work experience thrived, but students like me, used to lectures, found case study daunting.

Discussions proved intense, requiring hours of preparation each day. The professors divided us into study groups. Mine was composed of the silent ones of class: my roommate from Princeton, two Bobs from Dartmouth, and yours truly from the UW—Go Dawgs! We met after 10:00 p.m. and talked through the cases, finishing after midnight. We'd wake the next day around seven o'clock, breakfast at Kresge Hall, and be ready for battle by 8:40 a.m.

Early on, professors required us to compose a *written analysis of case* (WAC) every other Saturday, due by 5:00 p.m. Given the caseload and slow adaptation, I didn't have time to start until Friday night. Without word processors or Google then, I drew outlines and flow charts, often by hand. After little sleep and some quick oatmeal, I began pounding it out on my portable typewriter, praying for few typos.

Many Saturdays, I groaned to cheers from Soldiers Field, where Harvard played football against Ivy teams. I daydreamed about Husky football but kept on typing, often running to the WAC mailbox minutes before 5:00 p.m.

"Go, Murphy! Go!" classmates called out. They cheered and jeered us late arrivals at Baker Library, drinking beer and popping corn. Relieved yet exhausted, I escaped campus over the Charles to a pub called Charlie's Kitchen as my small reward.

"Steve, it's for you," Frank said, handing the phone to me one Sunday morning. We'd just had another debate about private versus public universities, our views polar opposites, like our East and West Coasts.

"Steve, this is Julia Casey, a friend of Pat Molloy of Seattle. We'd like you to come over for our family dinner," said Julia with a heavy Boston accent. I agreed, just to escape HBS.

"Welcome to our mad house. I'm Mama Julia," greeted an assertive lady, standing at five foot four. "Come into our humble abode."

Little did I know that this Irish Italian family, with seven lively kids, would become my safe zone on Sunday afternoons. Dinners highlighted my week, with explosive Mama Julia and demure husband, Bill, drawing smiles. Family discussions proved dramatic, yet I felt right at home.

I loved sharing my story with the Caseys, embellishing my tenure at HBS. I was "somebody" in this clan, not a "nobody" from the Pacific Northwest. I relished playing with their youngsters in their three-decker or strolling together through Dorchester's autumn leaves.

As Sunday afternoons came to an end, dread enveloped me on commute back on the T. Crossing the Charles River, I'd wistfully look back at Cambridge, as I approached HBS on the Boston side. I usually found Frank at his desk, preparing cases or joking about the Pacific Northwest. I tried to counter about the crowded East, but Ivy classmates didn't care. As I hailed well west of Manhattan, I felt of no account. So I turned back to the cases—those constant cases—preparing for Monday's debate.

Yet as I prepared for case discussions, self-doubt began gnawing my confidence. Although my hero JFK had attended Harvard, I questioned if this student from Seattle was meant to be here. At night, I tossed and turned at being called the next day, and I even dreamt of running away.

HBS professors were bright—some facetious—and charged to extract comment from each student. Their objectives were for us to have ah-ha moments, revealing key case precepts being discussed. The prof would guide discussion to such discovery, which we'd dub the "the golden glow," like the sun's reflection off Baker Library. Classroom debates came fast and furious, and I came prepared to avoid ridicule.

Eventually, we silent ones were called to analyze our cases, with the remaining students critiquing as company management. Frank and both Bobs responded well, if reluctantly, to the prof's entreaty. I offered a lackluster presentation compared to polished analyses of senior classmates. Only the tieless Mississippi student offered empathetic looks, unconcerned what others thought. Besieged, I looked at the clock, counting down till session's end.

After class, several Ivy students played flag football or threw Frisbee on the lawn. As for me, I found solace off campus, walking along the Charles toward the setting sun. The crews rowing in unison and cool breeze on my face offered respite from the hubbub of HBS.

On Sunday mornings, I played possum, not joining Frank across the river to St. Paul's Mass. Later, I'd feel guilty about backsliding and letting him down. So I hid in my bed, not wanting to rise—especially on weekdays. Yet HBS rigor got me up—whether I liked it or not—to continue another week. On the weekend, I called my mom, sharing my angst at HBS. "We believe in you," she often said, so I felt pressure to succeed, wrestling with their expectations and my growing despair. Yet I kept on keeping on, for Marian and Edward Murphy's son was not to quit!

Midterms appeared in early November in finance, marketing, and management. Using tools such as decision trees and golden glow concepts were encouraged. Frank usually left early, while the two Bobs and I turned in last. Afterward, I'd avoid Kresge and would walk along the Charles, amid disappointment and falling leaves.

Thanksgiving provided timely refuge. The Caseys invited me to dinner with three generations represented and took me to Plymouth Rock. I slept overnight on their couch and embraced them before returning on the T. I tried reading cases in the vacant dorm but walked again along the river, ending up at the Cambridge pub. I called my parents, who tried to cheer me up.

December's cold came in force, curtailing my odyssey along the river. Of the exams taken in October and November, we received grades from one course: I received a mere low pass plus and Frank a pass plus. Grades of other midterms were divulged in January. Inquiring about this delay, I was told that HBS tried to simulate stress and uncertainty of corporate life, to prepare us to manage with incomplete information. I heard talk of interlocking directorates between the Psychology Department and Business School but couldn't find out.

I just knew that HBS was grinding me down. I was not meeting the expectations of family and friends, let alone my own, so exalted mere months ago.

Hallelujah for Christmas break! I took my second cross-country flight across "America the Beautiful." As SeaTac came into misty view, I felt relief far away from HBS. My stalwart parents picked me up, driving home with few words. I went through the motions of the holiday season, avoiding friends. I walked our neighborhood and UW's campus—but did I still belong anymore?

"Stay the year at Harvard," my parents encouraged. "At least until summer."

I'd booked a flight in time for class but purposely delayed. Though I wanted to stay home, I knew my parents wished my return to HBS. The good-byes at the airport were poignant this time, my spirit drowning in pain.

Boston appeared bleaker—snow piling higher and the wind blowing fiercely. Traces of fall vanished—the ivy dying on the vine. The Charles had frozen, and pedestrians were scarce. The weather matched my dark mood as I trudged upstairs. My roommate quipped, "We thought you weren't returning, Murph." Well, I most reluctantly did, opening cases for the next day. Though I was away three weeks, it seemed much longer. When I studied myself in the mirror, more furrows creased my brow and less traces of a smile.

Whose reflection did I see—the me of Ivy expectations or the me of winter despair?

Classmates regarded me quizzically. My class performance continued to be mediocre, and November exams came rated low pass plus in finance and pass minus in marketing. For this UW graduate with distinction, the results were troubling—dare I even tell my parents? Where was my heady confidence of "*Je Pense, Donc Je Suis*"? Such thoughts tormented me in sleep, making me irritable and less confident.

The last week of January, I visited our section dean, Booth, a fellow Washingtonian. Booth was early in his career and offered empathy to this student of the Pacific Northwest. He'd later become governor of our state with positive reviews. His first words were "Welcome, Steve. I was wondering when you'd come in." I shared with him my distress and disappointment, which I'd refrained from sharing with classmates.

"I'm a fish out of water in the Ivy League," I confessed. "I hate HBS, and I'd like to leave. But my parents and sponsors want me to stay. What should I do? I don't see a way out!"

"Many students feel like you, Steve. But maybe you should seek another perspective," Booth counseled, suggesting HBS's psychiatrist. I thanked him for his time, but thought long about confiding in such a doctor—I'd never felt the need. I relented and set an appointment, mentioning to Frank that I had an outside meeting and would skip class. One did not skip classes at Harvard Business School.

The doctor seemed thoughtful, encouraging me to talk. I continued in a fog and regurgitated with less frankness and direction. He said that his door was always open and that I should find ways to release stress. I left his office but avoided Kresge, crossing over to Harvard College, seeking hopeful vibrations from undergrads. I returned that afternoon and found Frank looking askance. He knew something was up but didn't press. We prepared cases for the next day, the beginning of a new month.

I found sleep difficult, so picked up my diary, which I had begun at Harvard. I reread about my soaring expectations and the novelty that fall. I read about my winter of discontent and saw how low my spirit had fallen. I recalled not fitting in but how my folks willed me to succeed. My mood felt heavier, my dread of case discussions intense. I heard an owl hoot but saw no moon. On this last evening of January, I felt quite unsuccessful and wondered how this story would end. Thus, I penned a new entry:

An up-and-coming student went back East, to Harvard Business School—a bright future ahead. Yet when news broke that he'd taken his life, people at home expressed shock, asking, "Why did he do such a thing? He seemed such a promising young man." His sister, taken aback, perhaps asked, "Should I follow suit?" After all, her brother hadn't found happiness at school, nor had she. Maybe it was not to be?

So continued my late night ramblings, feeding an imagination in turmoil, as I fell into fitful sleep.

Stephen E. Murphy

Turning Point: "To Be or Not to Be—That Is the Question."

On February 2, I think the groundhog saw its shadow, suggesting six additional weeks of winter. I went to class that morning, thankfully not presenting before the class. I accompanied our silent ones to Kresge but picked at my food, excusing myself early. They asked where I was going, sensing that things weren't well. I said that I was taking a walk.

I left HBS and crossed the pedestrian bridge over the Charles. As I meandered alone, I looked over the edge and noticed a break in the ice. I studied that slight opening and wondered how long it'd take.

Being a reflective person, I toyed with this idea, turning north along the river's banks. I reached Memorial Bridge, and cars whizzed by. I stopped again to view the frozen river, wondering if my fall would break the ice. I ran briskly across oncoming traffic, barely noticing Newell Boathouse. Reversing course, I crossed the bridge to Boylston Street on the Cambridge side.

A creature of habit, I returned to Charlie's Kitchen, in search of liquid courage. I joined the regulars at the bar without comment. I nodded to the bartender, half listening to complaints about the Boston Bruins. Heavy thoughts returned, but was I ready to take that final step? I wondered what family and friends might think. But did I really care? Such was my despair. I wanted out of HBS, one way or another.

I left some bills on the counter and visited Harvard Square to say adios. The wind whistled and chased me down Mass Avenue. People regarded me oddly, so I looked away. In a haze, I reached Mount Auburn and saw St. Paul's down the street. I stopped and stared. Should I enter? Night had fallen, yet light shone through the doors—would I be welcome there? I took refuge from the cold.

Some parishioners were seated in this long, rectangular church, but I sat in the back pew. Its light was subdued, save a spotlight on the altar cross. I saw people kneeling, some praying. Toward the church's rear stood a traditional confessional, a light on the middle section, indicating a priest inside. As parishioners entered either side, the cubicle's light went off, indicating that someone was inside. I watched people going in and out until the cubicle closest to me showed a steady green. Should I dare go in? What would I say, but again, what did I have to lose?

I sat pondering, yet the light remained green—was it a sign? Slowly, I rose and went inside, kneeling down. A lattice grate separated the priest from the penitent. Inside, the priest had another sliding door, which remained closed while taking confession on the other side. I waited and thought to leave, as the priest hadn't opened his inner door. Maybe the person on the other side had a lot to confess too? The inner door finally opened, and I heard him say, "Bless you in the name of the Father, the Son, and the Holy Spirit. How long has it been since your last confession?"

"Well, Father, it's been more than two years—back when I lived in hometown Seattle, before coming to Harvard Business School."

He maintained his silence, as did I, but eventually he asked, "How may I help you, my son?"

Then all my anguish, disappointment, and sense of loss began to flow, breaking into a cascade of tears. I could not compose myself for a minute, and the patient priest said, "Tell me what's going on, my son."

So I began, sharing my early hopes and expectations at HBS, my disappointing academic performance, and my loss of confidence and sense of self.

"I've looked down at the Charles River, Father. My friends and family want me to do well at HBS, but I'm out of sync. I hate my life here. I don't know what to do. I just want out," I confessed.

Behind the lattice, I couldn't see him clearly but sensed attentiveness. Without interruption, he listened to my disjointed account until I'd run out of words. The priest took a pause and said these powerful words: "My son, my father died early in life. I didn't believe I'd recover from his passing. I was a very lost young man. But once a priest listened to me, as I am listening to you. Know that I am here not by chance. I believe that you have a future, which may not be clear now. Maybe it's not at Harvard but a future you have somewhere on earth.

"Pay attention to the little things in life—listen to the birds, feel the sun's warmth, smell a flower's bloom. Rest assured—you will find your path. And know that our Lord loves you, without condition, until the end of the world."

Again, the dam broke, and torrents of anguish left my being. Uncontrollably, I cried, until tears slowed to a smaller stream. After some moments, the priest asked me to say the Act of Contrition, which I couldn't remember. He asked me to say ten Our Fathers and ten Hail Marys outside, adding a final reminder and absolution. "Remember, my son, that Jesus loves you. He died on the cross so that you could live. Ask Him to show you the way. And I absolve you in the name of the Father, the Son, and the Holy Spirit," said this anonymous priest.

I thanked him, wavering at the confessional. I felt lighter and found a spot to kneel. I prayed in a broken manner, saying the ten Our Fathers and Hail Marys he'd asked me recite. I sat down and regarded Christ on the cross, pondering the priest's words. I sat there and didn't want to leave. Maybe there was hope, after all.

Then, the church lights turned brighter, and the evening Mass was about to begin. A lone soloist sang hymns, as acolyte and priest proceeded down the center aisle—was that he? I rose and mumbled through the liturgy and knelt for the consecration of bread and wine. Having confessed in earnest, I decided to take my first communion in years. A middle-aged priest put the body of Christ in my mouth; was that the priest who'd heard me out? I looked back, but he was offering communion to others. I walked down the side aisle, looking back again, and went outside.

It was a cold night, but it felt less harsh. I walked around Harvard Square and made my way to Charlie's Kitchen. The bartender nodded, saying, "You're back?" He knew I was going to Harvard somewhere and came for beer. I felt hungry and devoured a burger. Remembering the priest's words, I thought things might work out. I recrossed the Memorial Bridge, walking with more purpose.

"Where've you been, Murph?" Frank inquired.

"I went to Mass, Frank," I said sheepishly.

"What happened to you?"

"I guess it was about time," I affirmed, "and by the way, I've decided to leave HBS."

The following days went quickly, as did word around Section C. The silent ones were supportive, as well as the student from Mississippi. I reaffirmed my decision to Booth, who listened carefully, asking when I'd like to leave. "Why not St. Valentine's Day?"

He initiated the process to withdraw from HBS, the first one of Section C. I visited the registrar and received a check for $650. I bought a used Mercedes 219—my first and last so far in life. I called friends at Phi Kappa Psi fraternity's national office who asked, "We're planning to initiate a new colony in Portales, New Mexico. Would you like to join us?"

"Of course," I said, feeling better with somewhere to go.

I looked at the map and planned my cross-country trip. Only then did I call my mother to say I'd withdrawn from HBS. She was quiet at first and asked if I was sure. I said that it was right at this point in life and that I was going to help Phi Psi in New Mexico, travelling in my new Mercedes. She asked me to call often and speak with my father, which I did in a succinct manner.

February 14 was another cold but clear day in Boston. I'd asked Booth and our professor to speak with Section C students, and they'd agreed. Walking to class, I saw Baker Library's cupola, shining brightly, and entered class with Frank. The prof mentioned that I'd wanted to share a few words, so I swallowed and stood front and center.

I started slowly: "I appreciate the opportunity to attend HBS. Unfortunately, HBS was not the right place at this juncture of life. I have withdrawn. My action is not popular at home. Yet it is my declaration of independence. I've felt out of place, and I've lost confidence here. I needed to act."

The most silent of silent ones paused, then continued: "So I'm departing Harvard and all its promise, in pursuit of my path in life. It may not have the prestige of this institution nor the 'golden glow' we've come to know. Instead, my path will prove more elusive—something I'll call happiness."

I thanked them and saw classmates rising to their feet. I heard a "Rebel yell" from my "soul mate" from Mississippi and nods from Ivy Leaguers. I exited HBS into the bright morning sun and entered my Mercedes 219. I left Baker Library and its golden glow, behind in the rearview mirror.

I departed Boston quickly via I-95, through New York City traffic, and arrived in Philadelphia. I stayed at Penn's Phi Psi chapter and then drove through DC, where the Capitol shone brightly. I continued south to Virginia Tech for beer and BBQ with the brothers. The next day, I drove through West Virginia, seeing Charleston's capitol glowing in the sun.

How wonderful I felt on the road, getting lost or not—talking with the locals at chance encounters! When my Mercedes lost its distributor pin in rural Kentucky, the challenge proved therapeutic. Small things, such as hitching a ride from a farmer or chatting with the mechanic, grounded me in daily life. The mechanic, his son, and I shared stories over Kentucky white lightening, loosening our tongues.

"You know," I confessed. "I dropped out of grad school, and I'm afraid of what my parents may think."

"And how about you?" the mechanic inquired.

"I feel relieved—some disappointment," I replied, looking down.

"You got nothing to worry about, young man. Your folks love you as does the Lord above. Just keep on trucking, and you'll do fine!" he exclaimed, his teenage son nodding.

We then named my car Ursula in deference to her German roots and said, "So long." The bill he charged was five dollars, but the time together was priceless for my soul.

Eventually, I arrived at Vanderbilt University, after visiting Nashville's Grand Ole Opry in its original form. In the late morning, I shared buttermilk pancakes with sleepy students and travelled west to Fayetteville and then Austin. I crossed the Lone Star State, dodging tumbleweed, roadrunners, and cattle, bearing southwest. Slowly, HBS burdens lightened the farther west I travelled. Crossing over to Portales, I met brothers Hal and Phil at Eastern New Mexico University.

The brothers avoided mention of HBS but spoke about the type of student Phi Psi sought at this small state college: undergrads with GPAs over 3.5 and a spirit of adventure. At interviews, I spoke about my UW experience and how the fraternity broadened my horizons. We recruited six high-energy candidates and felt successful for our efforts.

I hit I-10 W., spending time on the Arizona and UCLA campuses. Promenading down Hollywood Boulevard, past Paramount Pictures, I wondered if I'd ever return. Up Highway One, I swallowed deeply, admiring the beautiful Pacific Ocean, so different from harsh Atlantic shores. At San Luis Obispo, I stayed at Cal Poly and body surfed the waves. I continued past charming Carmel to the city by the Bay.

A pledge brother attending Hastings Law lent me a sofa, catching up over Coronas. I finally spoke about my withdrawal, and John agreed the East Coast was *mucho* stuck up compared to our laid-back west. We listened to Jefferson Airplane, Dylan, and Baez railing against the war as the turntable went round and round.

Finally leaving San Francisco, I savored wines in Napa Valley and reached Eugene. I remember seeing a No Husky Zone sign, signaling the intense rivalry between our schools. I negotiated a sofa overnight at Oregon's chapter but left early next morning. The vibes in Duck country were unpleasant for this UW alum, so I hastened up I-5. Crossing the Columbia River, I breathed another sigh of relief. I made Seattle in three hours, adoring familiar sights—the Space Needle, Husky stadium, and Children's Orthopedic. I spotted Dad's Impala and Mom's Chevy in our driveway, and I released silent tears. Slowly but surely, my broken self was beginning to mend.

My dad answered the door, asking, "How's the traveler?" As a traveling salesman, my dad took me on business trips and sowed seeds of journey in his eldest son.

Around the Dunbar table, my parents and siblings asked about places visited and people met but thankfully avoided the big question. It was great seeing my brother, graduating in chemistry at the UW, and my sister, a graduating senior at Roosevelt High. My mom was her gracious self, advising that the family's EM Showrooms had relocated to Pioneer Square. That evening, I loved sleeping in my bed upstairs with my brother next door. I drifted off to a deep and restful sleep, home at last.

After lounging around, a former colleague at the Lazy B—local nickname for the Boeing Company—secured me a job at its aerospace division. I enjoyed the routine, continuing to recuperate into spring. Yet the Vietnam War soon touched Casa Murphy, as the draft board's letter reclassified me 1-A.

Like many graduates without student deferment, I had to think quickly what to do. I watched dismal news from Southeast Asia but spoke with Dad about where to serve. Like Mom, I was a swimmer, an aficionado of the sea. My dad counseled, "On board, you'll have a warm meal and a bed at night. It beats C rations in a foxhole."

I also sought out Fr. Fulton, nicknamed Fr. Joy, who'd served as my confirmation priest. I spoke about the anonymous priest who'd heard me out and offered a special prayer. I also asked Fr. Joy for his advice, but he said to choose the path, which felt right in my heart.

With the clock ticking down, I applied to Officer Candidate School (OCS) in the US Navy and received response mid-June. The navy had accepted me as a candidate for the incoming class of October 1967. My vacation was officially over.

CHAPTER 2
Vietnam

PROTESTS NATIONWIDE ERUPTED against the war, including at the UW and on I-5. Dad and Mom supported my decision to serve our country, and that's what mattered to me. As I prepared my bags for the navy's Officer Candidate School in Newport, my sister, Pamela, packed hers for the UW's rival, WSU at Pullman. My brother, Terry, was pursuing his PhD in chemistry—more terrifying than Vietnam to me.

My mother practiced swimming to cross Lake Washington in the renowned Fatty Fleet race—I felt proud. Dad soared above us all in his Cessna, visiting clients throughout the Pacific Northwest. I admired his adventurous spirit, wanting to follow in my own way.

Labor Day came, and we celebrated summer's end at the beach club and I took another jump off the tower. We said our good-byes amid hugs and expectations, soon going our respective ways.

Ursula was my great companion until Newport's gate, when the marine guard pointed to the parking lot where the chief petty officer (CPO) barked at incoming candidates. "You're in the navy now! We plan to square away you sorry-looking civilians. If not, off to the fleet you go." This proverbial bulldog went up and down the line, rebuking our "sorry" look, making me smile.

"Give me thirty, cadet," he charged me and, when complete, marched us inside the OCS gates. I picked up blue dungarees, shirts, darker blues, and black shoes before I sought my room—my new home away from home. I paired up with a Tennessee grad, looking more squared away than me.

We stored our gear and mustered again to the CPO's favorite melody, "You're in the Navy Now." I knew the song from old TV shows, but here it was for real—no sitcom now! Our reward at day's end was the navy's barber, watching our locks fall away. I looked at my new look, muttering, "I'm in the navy now."

The daily routine was constant, unless I got demerits. At 0600 were reveille, calisthenics, and cleanup; 0700 was for breakfast room inspection. At 0745, we were in the classroom, had chow at noon, and were back to classes at 1300. And drills began at 1530.

My bed had to be made perfectly taut, with square corners. If not, the CPO gave out demerits, landing me to clean urinals on weekends. If I got more than thirty demerits or made an enemy of the CPO, then "off to the fleet" I'd go!

Academics emphasized mathematics, navigation, and leadership. I studied up—what else was there to do? OCS's four months went by in a blur, but even today I shiver, remembering the wind off Narragansett Bay.

Whenever Ursula cooperated, I'd drive cadets to the Caseys, who seemed in awe of us, dressed in naval blues. Julia was firmly against the war, and patriarch Bill raised historical questions. Despite different views, Sunday dinner at Casa Casey still proved my safety zone. CBS's Walter Cronkite gave us pause as war coverage turned bloodier and protests ramped up.

I counted down the days and requested my duty assignment after graduation. For my ship, I chose a destroyer, frigate, or riverine boat. And for my billet, I chose gunnery, fire control, or combat information. For home port, I selected San Diego, Pearl Harbor, or Subic Bay, figuring the navy would send me to Southeast Asia anyway.

At the time, I believed that the United States was doing right to protect the South Vietnamese against aggressors from the north. I'd seen us on the brink before, during the Cuban Missile Crisis, Congo, and Berlin. In

Vietnam, war was becoming hotter. I swallowed hard, put my hand on the Bible, pledging to do my duty to protect our nation and the Constitution.

March 8 arrived—graduation day! All but one of Papa Company were commissioned ensigns, US Navy Reserve, and we threw our covers in the air. Holding my breath, I stopped by the commandant's office for orders, which read, "Report to USS *Goldsborough*, DDG 20, Pearl Harbor, Hawaii. Billet, Gunnery and Missile Officer; Leave, seven days."

I was truly "in the navy" now!

The Caseys joined my parents to celebrate at Newport's finest inn. Ursula, however, blew her head gasket, pumping out high-pressure steam. My dad chuckled at my locomotive, but followed in my wake. At the used-car dealership, my Mercedes 219 was ignominiously traded for a used '64 Chevy II.

We Murphys and Caseys had a bittersweet luncheon—the ladies giving hugs and the men shaking hands. Our three cars parted in different directions, and I hoped that I'd see them again.

Solo, I raced cross-country and arrived in time to ship Ursula II, courtesy of the US Navy, to Hawaii. I found Alameda's Naval Air Station and took off after midnight. I viewed the Golden Gate Bridge below and hoped OCS's training had prepared me for the war ahead.

At dawn, we circled Pearl Harbor and the Arizona Memorial, landing at Barbers Point. I shuttled into Pearl to *Goldsborough*'s pier, admiring the 437-foot guided-missile destroyer roll before the trade winds. At 0800, I saluted the flag and the officer of the deck (OOD), reporting for duty. The executive officer (XO) arrived, looking me up and down. He showed me quarters with two other ensigns and a warrant officer, currently on the beach. He suggested changing into the correct uniform of tropical whites and pointed toward the post exchange. In my navy blues, I received lots of stares, as this newly minted ensign tried to find his way.

Later, I met roommates Lex, USNR ensign from Jersey; Bob, USN ensign from Annapolis; and Ron, warrant from Philadelphia. "A salt of the earth," Ron rose through the ranks and served as fire control officer (FCO). We'd become close shipmates, as the FCO and gunnery officer worked hand in hand. Fire control fed data, like ship, wind, and current speeds and direction into mainframe computers to determine at which angle to direct the five-inch guns and missile launcher, which were under my command.

In the wardroom, the XO introduced the commanding officer (CO), a career USN commander with eighteen years of service. He'd gone to the US Naval Academy and bonded with regular officers like Bob. My commission was from US Navy Reserve, not the prestigious USN. The CO seemed formal but welcomed me aboard with caveats: "Take good care of those 5"/54 guns, Mr. Murphy. They'll save our bacon in Vietnam. Get to know your chief."

Gunnery's chief was a sixteen-year "salt," boasting mechanical and sailor skills. Chiefs onboard provided *Goldsborough*'s human backbone, garnering rapport with three hundred enlisted men. I'd have to learn on my feet as division officer and hoped I had the stuff.

At OCS, I was taught to maintain an aloof manner toward enlisted men and to lead by example. The wardroom was center of the ship's officer corps, and it was the site for breakfast, lunch, and dinner. The CO presided over the table of thirteen officers, each seated by seniority. As junior officer (JO), I sat at the end and didn't speak unless spoken to. Verbal exchanges were usually short, not sweet, as the CO often asked JO's to expound on subjects of his choosing. The wardroom was our information center, where we'd glean unofficial knowledge as well as the CO's state of mind.

On the high seas, the CO's word was absolute. Recalling *Mutiny on the Bounty*, I hoped we didn't have another Captain Bligh.

To prepare for deployment, the squadron commander required rigorous training of ships under his command. *Goldsborough* cruised independently to improve on-board training but also in squadron with other ships. Our CO was tense whenever the commodore critiqued each ship. If we didn't perform to the CO's standards, he'd rail against the XO, department head, or junior officer in charge. I'd cringe upon hearing, "Mr. Murphy to the bridge." I'd say "Yes sir" to my chewing out, while the OOD and enlisted men stood watch, pretending not to listen.

In the gunnery division, three units reported to the chief. Of eighteen enlisted men, most came from the South or small-town America, representing all races. They'd been without an officer for fourteen months and were curious about the new ensign—was he a hard ass or not? I had to get up to speed ASAP.

As gunnery officer, my collateral duty was to prepare the ship's landing party. Since the Civil War, landing parties were trained to enter a combat zone if called. In peacetime, landing parties were mostly untrained, but in Vietnam, things changed.

"Ensign Murphy, I want a trained landing party. No shrinking violets on my ship!" the CO commanded.

So I took the charge to heart and recruited gung-ho volunteers. They joked that it'd be fun training outdoors and shooting M16s. I organized field trips in the hustings of Maui, Kauai, and the Big Island, overnighting in the woods. One night, guys from the South heard a wild pig rooting and chased it, machetes drawn. Such incidents garnered our name, Murphy's Marauders. Afterward, members strutted proudly on the ship.

Goldsborough had final drills, tweaking guns and equipment. We practiced general quarters (GQ), when each mariner went to specific stations and had specific tasks to do. GQ was called if the ship was threatened. "Serious business," I said to myself and climbed to the gun director, the highest point of the ship. My duty was to direct gunfire optically, if the ship was under attack. For naval gunfire support, I'd use the optical reader to spot the target and then hand it off to fire control.

The sailors seemed quieter then, paying close attention to detail. *Goldsborough* was about to cross the Pacific Ocean—to the other side. I hoped to meet the challenge under fire.

No shore leave was permitted as we prepared for deployment. We sailed on October's dawn with two destroyers to rendezvous at Midway, the site of WWII's famous battle. Outside the war zone, watch condition was set one in four, or four hours on watch and twelve hours off, to attend duties onboard.

Stephen E. Murphy

As gunnery officer, I met with my division every morning at quarters, when the CO inspected and announced itinerations for the day. When dismissed, I'd meet our men to pass additional word from the wardroom. The chief delivered work assignments, and I inspected ordnance, gauging sailor moods as well. I liked this routine but sensed it was about to change.

Underway, my watch duty was on the bridge with the OOD as junior officer of the deck, along with the helmsman, navigator, radar operator, and lookouts on each wing. The CO often sat in his captain's chair, observing the sea, our formation, and our performance. On my first midwatch—from midnight to 0400—we cruised at twenty knots, the bow waves revealing ocean phosphorescence. That bridge watch at night offered solace from daily routine. I appreciated its serenity. Sometimes, the OOD asked me to tour the ship, ensuring blackout conditions—especially in war zones.

Steaming in formation with other ships, the JOOD and OOD paid special attention. We took bearings on neighboring ships and observed their running lights. When radar shouted, "constant angle—diminishing range," we'd fear a collision course forthcoming. We'd radio the other ship's OOD to see what was going on. Occasionally, we took evasive action in extremis. I was always on guard at night—sailors' lives were at stake.

When my relief officer arrived prior to the watch's end at 0350, I'd explain it like this: "We're steaming in formation, *Goldsborough* on port flank. Course is 250. Speed is twenty knots, wind from the north, swells at seven feet. Notify the Captain any course change. ETA Midway, 0900."

After the officer understood the tactical and maritime situation, he'd say, "I relieve you," to which I'd reply, "I stand relieved." I left the bridge to my stateroom, crashing on the top bunk, until the IMC announced, "Reveille." At Midway, we replenished fuel and stores, amusing ourselves at gooney birds' antics. At dusk, the squadron departed with two guided-missile destroyers, two destroyers, a destroyer escort, and a frigate, where the squadron commander posted his flag. We sailed in a southwesterly direction with fair winds and following seas.

After a quiet cruise, we reached the war zone in the South China Sea. Our squadron was assigned to escort the carrier USS *Hancock*. Strategically, destroyers provided screen to the capital ship from any hostile attack. Destroyers were thus expendable to enemy threats as long as they protected the carrier or battle ship. We went to readiness state, port and starboard, with six hours on watch—myself in the gun director—and six hours off, to perform regular duties and maybe to sleep. During this state, most of the crew was sleep deprived—nerves taut, tempers flaring.

The closer we approached the war zone, the more nervous our CO became. My roommate Lex had uncanny ability to deflect the CO's concerns. An RPI graduate in engineering, he knew his stuff. I envied Lex's people skills, but my strategy was to avoid the bridge.

After carrier duty, *Goldsborough* patrolled the demilitarized zone between North and South Vietnam. Our usual mission required naval gunfire support, helping marines on the ground against North Vietnamese Army, or NVA. The marine spotter would identify the target, such as an enemy platoon; give its coordinates; and suggest the type of projectile to use. Fire control would then relay the solution to gunnery, loading high-explosive shells against enemy troops. When ready, I ordered, "Fire for effect!"

If the shell didn't hit the target, the spotter would say something like, "Right one hundred meters, up one hundred fifty." When a target's coordinates were unclear, I'd seek it atop the gun director, trying to lock on our radar and hand it to fire control for solution.

Historically, the US Navy worked closely with the US Marine Corps (USMC) from the "halls of Montezuma to the shores of Tripoli." On capital ships, marine troops were stationed to protect the ship against enemy boarders or mutineers aboard. In Vietnam, the USMC had their own chain of command but worked closely with their sister service to support moves on the ground.

In the DMZ, there were large-scale firefights between the NVA and the USMC, over strategic hills described in Karl Marlantes's *Matterhorn*. Such hills would pass from one side to another over several campaigns. I often followed the firefights atop my ship, appreciating again Dad's advice.

Our sixty-one days offshore were about to end. *Goldsborough* was granted a week of R & R in Hong Kong. I detected snappier salutes from sailors, who painted over ship battle scars. We headed northeast to this British Crown colony, with old salts recounting tales of lore.

I stared in awe when Hong Kong came into sight—its beauty stunning. The CO took the conn on entering the harbor, guided by the pilot to our berth. The pilot avoided shoals, sampans and ferries plying its waters, and headed toward Kowloon, past the majestic Peninsula Hotel.

The CO took a couple tries to dock *Goldsborough* alongside an Aussie frigate, its CO frowning from the bridge. I made sure my uniform was pressed for the captain's inspection, eager to hit the beach. As junior ensign, however, I drew duty and imagined the fun ashore, ogling Hong Kong by night.

We were charged to return by 0800 to avoid being absent without leave. For whoever missed morning muster, "a captain's mast" was likely, the tardy sailor "put in hack" and future liberty withdrawn. Before the captain's inspection began, we put on our best uniforms and nursed hopes for a great time on the "beach."

The next night, I went ashore with Lex and Ron, riding the Star ferry to Hong Kong. A veteran officer led us to his favorite dim sum, looking raunchy and smelling of garlic. Its shrimp dumplings were scrumptious, so I gobbled them down over beer. The officer extolled the delights of Wan Chai, whose bars never closed. Feeling no pain, I exited to the night.

I wandered into a red lit bar, blaring "In a Gadda da Vida," with servicemen drinking and dancing as if there were no tomorrow. At the bar, I met Nancy, who smiled and said, "Buy me a drink." I did so and followed her down the street. Her English was broken, but her appeal was great to this sailor of the line. I barely arrived for muster at 0800.

In port, navy techs fixed one of our guns, which had been jamming. On board, the crew was upbeat, with sailors responding with smiles or remarks like, "Mr. Murphy, we understand you had fun on the beach."

"Go along to get along," I said to myself, reveling in this R & R port. I asked for—and received—two days of leave and returned to Nancy, inviting her to nice restaurants at Victoria's Peak.

The day before departure, she took me home in Fanling, with a gray view of the Peoples Republic of China. She introduced her mother, who bowed often and made us tea. She spoke in Cantonese with Nancy, who smiled and said, "She thinks you look very American." She confided that her family had escaped down the Pearl River three years ago and "liked Hong Kong's nightlife."

Hand in hand, she led me to the bus for Kowloon, bowing slightly. I entered the bus, and she looked back once and, with a wave, climbed up the hill. The people onboard looked askance at this *gweilo*, or "ghost devil." I looked away, daydreaming about my time with this perky Chinese maiden. I never saw Nancy again but started receiving letters later that year.

Onboard, the mood became somber. Nourishing R & R memories, we exchanged tales of Wan Chai. Everyone but one arrived by 0800, preparing psychologically to return to the line of battle. Later, the AWOL sailor was picked up by the military police in a bar fight, put in cuffs, and sent back to the fleet. The captain busted him down one rank and suspended his leave for the cruise.

We returned to the Gulf of Tonkin to support the marines in the DMZ. According to a friend on the bridge, the CO received a call from a USMC colonel about the "state of *Goldsborough*'s landing party." The CO report-edly said, "Ensign Murphy has a trained landing party and is ready to go." I was not party to this exchange, but on hearing "Away the landing party," I felt shock. It was unusual to call the landing party, except in an emergency.

In Hawaii, the dozen Murphy's Marauders thought it a bit of a lark, with field trips and gun practice on the range. After the 1MC order, moods changed abruptly, realizing this was not a drill. The ship's armorer brought vintage Browning Automatic Rifles and M1s, two M14s, a Tommy gun, and of course, the .45 pistol for the officer in charge.

Silently, we prepared the whaleboat with gear and life preservers. The petty officer in charge was looking glum. The sailors felt secure onboard, but uncertain ashore. "That's for jar heads," they'd often joke. No lon-ger were we joking, looking down at eight-foot swells. I then heard, "Mr. Murphy, report to the bridge. Secure the landing party."

Relief was painted on sailor faces, though I felt disappointment, hoping to witness our party in action. Later, a braggart said how he "wanted to kill Cong," looking away when he saw me. I recalled his gray look when the boat was ready to depart. On the bridge, the CO congratulated our fast turnaround, ecstatic with the colonel's "Bravo Zulu," for well done. The USMC secured the beach with their own.

After this excitement, we returned to duty stations. Atop the director, I looked toward the beach where the landing party would have disembarked. I saw puffs of smoke and trained the director's optics, seeing marines run for cover—they were under attack. We soon got a call, giving coordinates of the NVA's 105 mm rocket launcher. I said, "Fire for effect." Guided by fire control's solution, the five-inch guns "walked up" rounds to enemy ordnance. After five salvos, the spotter shouted "Bravo Zulu," and the puffs ceased. *Hmmm*, I thought, *that could have been us.*

After this dust up, *Goldsborough* was tasked to help troops under siege at Chu Lai after Tet's offensive. Ground forces appreciated our can-do spirit. The gray ghost, as they called us, was in high demand.

At night, I recalled weird light shows, starring "Puff, the Magic Dragon," the super helicopter gunship. In "The *Goldsborough* Report," for Phi Kappa Psi's *Shield* in 1969, I wrote:

You see Puff stick its draconian tongue at unfortunate souls, its Gatling gun like Satan's laser from above. Tracers fence their way across sand dunes. Its guns commence Act II. The star shells and multicolor flares form their kaleidoscope amongst celestial bodies. Gun flashes silhouette adjacent hills, answered down the coast. Junks pass and stony-faced fishermen ride out the storm, bobbing in the wake of this forty-five-hundred-ton man-of-war. Thus, you conclude another night on the line…as morning light breaks the dawn.

Yet in quieter moments, I often wondered about those unfortunate souls. Despite our mission to support brothers in arms, I had doubts. On Sunday services on the fantail, we prayed to keep our troops safe and to protect civilians caught in war's crossfire. Afterward, I'd hear tell of another friend ashore killed in action. The war became personal again, and I put my questions back in the box, not to reopen until I'd left the USN.

After forty-five days at sea, we exited south past the Mekong Delta, en route to another R & R. We entered the Chao Phrya River, and I heard "I love Bangkok" from the crew. I admired pagoda palaces and golden roofs of *The King and I*, as the *Goldsborough* avoided watercraft of all sizes, docking without mishap. Each person had duty one night on, the next off, for six days in port—R & R was about to rock and roll.

Again, I drew duty but enjoyed dinner with two officers from the Royal Thai Navy. They were quiet compared to us boisterous Americans but enjoyed our camaraderie. I sat next to a Thai ensign, who said that he was about to marry later in the week, inviting me to attend.

The following night, I joined junior officers, wandering through Bangkok's crooked streets. I followed others into the Honey Hotel and savored hotsy baths of soft touches and warm water running down my back.

The Thai ensign sent me a formal invitation Saturday, to which I agreed after receiving my CO's approval: "Maybe you should consider the diplomatic corps, Ensign Murphy."

A naval escort awaited and navigated through Bangkok streets, winding like its river. He drove on the left side of the road, like in London or Tokyo, dodging pedestrians and animal carts. He dropped me off at an ornate hall with a long line waiting to speak with the bride and groom.

"Where will the wedding ceremony be?" I inquired.

The escort replied, "This is the ceremony. Each guest should provide the couple with counsel for a happy marriage. After the visitors have shared, this couple is considered married. This is our Buddhist way."

I shared few words but many smiles with guests from Thailand's navy. Reaching my new friend and his lovely bride, I wished them dialogue in good times and in bad. We all toasted this couple, resplendent in white and fulsome smiles. We offered *namaste* to them, their families, and their nuptial vows.

Reluctantly, I bid the couple adieu, returning to the gray ghost. R & R was winding down. Underway at dawn, we transited through the Gulfs of Thailand and Tonkin for escort duty again. After twenty days, one gun acted up, cutting our mission short.

We cruised through the South China Sea and arrived Kaohsiung. I stayed onboard to fix "bad boy" mount fifty-two, replacing its loading gear. Taiwan's port seemed less exotic than Bangkok, but it did sell knock-off long plays at three for a dollar.

Our next port of call was Sasebo Naval Base, on Kyushu in Japan. I took leave and a fast train to Nagasaki, visiting two hills of martyrs—the first was to honor victims from WWII's atomic bomb, while the second was to honor twenty-six Portuguese priests, crucified by the shogun in 1597 for spreading the Christian faith. At both sites, I caught stares from townspeople but bowed my head in reflection.

Word came that the *Goldsborough* was finally heading home. I joined the crew to cheer, readying the ship in record time. I heard whistling on the deck—and not just from the boatswain mate. We stood one watch on, three off, and settled into easy routine, heading southeast.

On the bridge, I saw flying fish and hammerhead sharks as we entered subtropical waters. Six snouts were poking the surface, looking for prey. I shuddered and was grateful I didn't have to take our whaleboat into open sea that day.

I stood watch before a fiery dawn and recalled, "Red in the morning, sailors take warning; red at night, sailor's delight." Within an hour, clouds rumbled in from the north with wave swells reaching twenty feet. Skies darkened at 0730, and the seas doubled to forty feet. I shuddered as we surfed the waves but stared at a monster fifty footer, dead ahead. We took the wave on our port bow, plunging deep into the sea. Green water covered the bridge, and I grabbed the helmsman to stay the course. Would this typhoon ever end? It was more terrible than Vietnam.

The ship rolled violently, and I hung on for dear life. I tied the helmsman to the wheel and tightened hatches to keep water out. After thirty minutes in a perilous state, the sea gave a slight respite. The swells dropped to thirty feet but had force to roll the ship. After an hour, the waves only reached twenty feet, giving me confidence that we'd survive. That day, I earned new respect of the sea's power. I also said a prayer.

Using radar to navigate "the soup," we spotted Midway's channel buoys and gooney birds to guide us in. Per naval tradition, sailors and officers alike had to clean up lost lunches from the storm: rank hath no privilege on this duty, including Ensign Murphy.

Morning skies appeared pink, and I hoped for a smoother return. We entered up the slot at Pearl, creeping by Ford Island. Dressed in whites, we presented handsome profiles to wives, families, and friends donning leis ashore. The USS *Goldsborough*, after eight months offshore of Vietnam, returned to port. Sailors moved swiftly to cast lines ashore. We'd finally arrived home!

The ship was slated for dry dock so new ordnance and boilers could be installed. As it would take several months to complete, Lex, Quince, and I decided to set up our "snake ranch," as bachelor pads were called.

My boss, Quince, the weapons officer, was fun to be around. His irreverence toward authority in private was renowned. From Southern California, he loved the navy, if not the CO. After the war, he found his way to Thailand, leading a life of mystery. We're surprisingly connected via LinkedIn.

We found an apartment overlooking the Ala Wai Canal, within walking distance of Waikiki. On Sunday afternoons, we'd frequent the Royal Hawaiian's happy hour. The mai tais were strong and inexpensive, encouraging talk with *wahines* and tales of the western Pacific. On return to the pad, I'd sometimes drop a blinking traffic horse into the pool, making a big splash Sunday night.

Socially, I attended luaus, where whole pigs, wrapped in banana leaves and roasted underground on steaming rocks, offered succulent treats. A Chinese

Hawaiian shipmate invited me to a family luau and, over mai tais, shared his philosophy: "In Hawaii, we're able to laugh at ourselves. We joke without taking offense. We Hawaiians keep balance with humor and tell jokes about each other—Polynesians, Samoans, Japanese, Filipinos, Chinese, and Anglos—but always with a smile on our face."

Entering 1970, the CO interviewed all JOs of the US Navy Reserve. I was now lieutenant junior grade, while Lex was a lieutenant. Quince was promoted to lieutenant commander, USN, and was considered a lifer. He proved them wrong six years later when he exited for his odyssey in Southeast Asia.

The captain called me in and asked my plans.

"I'd like to return and finish my MBA," I replied.

"Maybe a diplomat?" he said, inquiring. "Would you like to exit in July rather than wait until next year?"

"Yes sir," I replied.

"By the way, I have a diplomatic duty for you as liaison officer for a Brazilian training ship. You speak some languages, like Spanish and Portuguese, I understand?"

"Yes sir," I said, happy in my modest diplomatic mission.

Lieutenant Noce greeted me in Portuguese, sharing enchanting stories of Rio's Copacabana. He had an easy manner and wandering eyes, appreciating our snake ranch over mai tais. He was the CO's nephew and had secured posting on this worldwide tour. He charged me to invite Waikiki *wahines*, and his ship would host a Brazilian carnival for the *Goldsborough*. Concluding my "diplomatic mission" onboard his ship, we danced the samba until late. Even my CO confessed this was the "liveliest party" he'd ever attended: "Maybe you have a future after all, Mr. Murphy!"

With my early out in the works, I reapplied to Columbia Business School, receiving acceptance again, including advance credit for HBS courses. Quince and Lex encouraged me to finish my MBA and to "get out while the getting was good."

However, I almost didn't make it. One Saturday morning, I agreed to snorkel with a shipmate off Makaha, Oahu's northwest point. He didn't show, so I dove in alone in search of tropical fish. I spotted a mahi mahi, chasing it beyond twenty feet, forgetting to equalize pressure. Suddenly, my right ear popped, and the world spun around. As water penetrated my inner ear, I lost my balance and felt upside down. The ocean bottom's sand reflected light from above. It was hard to gauge which way was up.

I stopped. Then I followed my body trending upward and broke the surface in choppy waters. I somehow swam ashore, climbed up rocks, and drove my Chevy II in unsteady state. I arrived at the infirmary, spending a hard night with a throbbing ear.

Was there a reason that I was spared again? Was someone upstairs looking out after all? I reflected on my fearless actions yet hoped that Vietnam had grounded me for my next chapter in life.

CHAPTER 3

Columbia Business School

MOUNT RAINIER EMERGED through clouds, and I felt at home. The cabbie muttered about the rain, leaving me at my parents' showroom in Pioneer Square. "You look great in your navy whites," they said—I always yearned for their approval. They were pleased at my reacceptance to Columbia Business School and toasted my return.

At Sand Point Naval Air, I separated from the USN, opting out of active reserves. I attended my brother's wedding, where he chose a brother in faith for his best man over his brother on the loose. I felt disappointment but wished them well. Transitioning to a civilian world, I hoped I'd adjust with shipmates still at risk.

A fellow navy vet, Christopher Bayley, declared for prosecuting attorney, battling an entrenched GOP incumbent. He had a "clean government" message, so I decided to help out. With campaign workers, I'd share war stories. But their eyes glazed over, reminding this returning vet to keep his peace. Americans were tired of Vietnam.

Learning of my journey to Columbia, a neighbor asked if I'd deliver her sister's Lemans to New York City. I agreed on the spot and found a UW student named Rory to share the cross-country drive. A Londoner, he was intent on teaching me the Queen's English.

"Good luck, son," wished my parents.

"I'll do my best," I promised, hoping not to disappoint. We barreled across I-90 and reached beautiful Boise at dusk. We continued to Jackson Hole and Yellowstone, admiring Old Faithful at the lodge. "So this is how they talk American," he said on reaching Rapid City. We both admired the town folk, who spoke plainly, residing in homes surrounded by grassy yards. Unhindered by fences, it was like one big community park.

In Madison, I asked Phi Psi's for a couch overnight. The badger brothers obliged: "As long as you join us for Bud!"

I did, but my English traveler complained about "hops and water," opting for Guinness. We bypassed Chicago's urban sprawl and reached Youngstown's steel mills, eating BBQ with workers. I sped east on I-80, tiring of his English lessons until I said, "Enough!" We followed signs into New York City, like homing pigeons to the hood.

"Stay in the car," I ordered and double-parked outside Phi Kappa Psi. Inside, I spoke with the manager, Victor, who said all rooms were taken. "But I'm a brother Phi Psi from Washington," I implored. "Surely I could overnight on this empty couch?" He smiled and agreed. Victor brightened when he saw Rory, offering us a joint to boot.

"No, thanks. But we'd love a burger," I replied. He pointed toward the popular Gold Rail, where I passed antiwar demonstrators and bit my tongue. Was I really prepared for civilian life in all its messy form?

The next morning, I called my neighbor's sister, asking if I should drive to Bronxville or meet her in Manhattan. "Why not join me at the Tavern on the Green?" she suggested, and I readily agreed. Victor seemed upbeat midmorning, so I pressed my luck for another night. He smiled and said sure, again.

I walked Rory to the subway to JFK, wishing him, cheerio. "You're finally learning the Queen's English, mate," he quipped. On Amsterdam Avenue, I found the Lemans without scratches and breathed a sigh of relief. I drove it to the trendy tavern just off of Central Park West, leaving it with the valet.

"You must be Steve," affirmed this forty-something woman, dressed in a chic, pink pantsuit. "Welcome to the big city," she offered over a three-course lunch. I consumed it as elegantly as possible, despite my hungry state. Her name was Mrs. Robinson, so I wondered what'd be next. Disappointment on my face, she dropped me off at Columbia's gates, waving and continuing uptown to her suburban estate.

This second time through Columbia's campus, I admired *Alma Mater*, its hallmark statue standing guard. I shook my head at antiwar graffiti near Uris Hall but entered to register finance as my MBA concentration. The attendant looked me over when I asked about a place to stay, raising an eyebrow and hollering, "Next?"

Campus housing was closed, but shared apartments were listed at $150–$500 a month. Back at Phi Psi's rooming house, Victor continued smoking weed and announced, "Steve's a real Phi Psi from Washington," asking if I'd like a hit.

"*Porque no?*" I replied, and they laughed at my *español*. I remember little, save Victor's question about living in what he called a "closet." I repeated, "Why not?"

Hanging onto shaky bannisters, we climbed up five creaky floors. The closet, a six-by-eight-foot room with a skylight, sported few amenities but several roaches. Still, I shook hands with Victor, paying twenty-five dollars for my monthly rent. It beat the street.

Duly registered and secure in my closet, I looked forward to grad school. Despite protests and unstructured living, Columbia somehow felt right from the start. At local taverns, I chatted with students from all over the world and enjoyed seeing Upper West Side coeds strolling by.

Saturday, I ran into a student from São Paulo, Samy, who asked, "*Tudo bem?*" or "All well?" I replied in limited Portuguese but accepted his invite for espresso at the Hungarian pastry shop. "Our place is a zoo," he opined, "but they don't hassle you."

"But what about me, as a veteran?" I inquired. "It seems hostile around here."

"Just keep that to yourself," he advised, "and everything will be fine." He was finishing his fourth year at Columbia College in communications and relished New York's bohemian lifestyle.

On Monday morning, I returned for orientation and classes—corporate finance, marketing, operations research, and international business. Classes took place in twelve-story Uris Hall, space at a premium at Columbia and in Manhattan. In my classroom, I counted thirty-five students, including ten international and four women—twice as many as in HBS. Columbia felt great to me, with students of all walks of life, in contrast to the citadel of the Ivy League.

Another comfort zone at Columbia was its mix of lecture and case studies. I teamed with international students—from Mexico, Venezuela, Pakistan, Belgium, and France—for case analyses and presentations. Often, we'd discuss over lunch at the Cuban Chinese hole-in-the-wall discovered on my first foray down Broadway. That semester, I paced myself without feeling overwhelmed and received B plusses and A minuses on midterms—what a difference from HBS!

To be fair, I was three years older than at HBS and had survived a war zone. Dodging fire and typhoons shored up my confidence. If I made it through Vietnam, I could navigate grad school. I was helped by naval discipline, time management skills and the GI bill too. At Columbia, I felt less pressure and spent time with students from south of the border I loved living in a city that never sleeps and planned outings beyond Manhattan's borders.

Convincing classmates to venture to Brooklyn's Academy of Music, we stopped by a UW grad's townhouse near Prospect Park en route to *El Ballet Folklorico de Mexico*. My UW friend John enjoyed telling us hair-raising tales from the USSR over Russian vodka. He travelled to Moscow with frequency and had a grand repertoire. After Brooklyn, I'd venture to another borough—this time the Bronx!

My blind date was a friend of a friend from Puerto Rico. I struggled locating her project on Grand Concourse, which was like scenes from *The Bonfires of the Vanities*. Celia thanked me for coming and led me through groups of teens hanging out. If someone gave her lip, she'd erupt in Spanish and English, causing them to back off—no one messed with Celia! We saw *The Harder They Come*, sang reggae, and had a good time. I bid her, "*Hasta luego*," found the Number 2 subway to Grand Central Station, exiting at W. 125th—not a good idea at 2:00 a.m. Among catcalls, I walked briskly by Harlem's basketball courts and jogged up Morningside Heights, arriving at home sweet home. I wondered if Vietnam had helped me lose my fear.

That semester, I made the dean's list, regaining confidence that I could perform academically. To commemorate, I threw my first rooftop party in March, as New York had an early spring. I invited roommates and Columbia friends, including students from an intercultural retreat. Polish American Lucja livened up both the retreat and the party, enjoying my rendition of rum punch. Even my former HBS roommate, Frank, appeared from his showbiz gig, enjoying the West Side's potpourri.

My classmate Allan came to extol AIESEC internships over punch. As the Columbia chapter's president, he encouraged me to apply. Inspired by the Marshall Plan in 1948, AIESEC encouraged business-student exchanges between the United States and Europe. Today, AIESEC is the largest student exchange organization in 110 countries. In 1971, it placed most students in Europe and some in Latin America.

The spring semester was really fun. I took Latin American development at the School of International and Public Affairs, taught by renowned economist Raul Prebisch. I met his sharp assistant, Dr. Enrique, who'd later become a friend and the president of the Inter-American Development Bank. I did well that semester but wondered about the summer. Several students sought internships on Wall Street, but I felt called south of the border.

In *Business Week*, I read about BankBoston's VP of Brazil who'd completed management contracts to triple his bank network. That seemed enterprising, so I wrote him in São Paulo, sending kudos but asking for a job. I also wrote its Boston VP of Latin America and scoured magazines for opportunities, spying one in Managua. A Nicaraguan cautioned that I'd be working for a dictator's family and should take care. I wrote anyway, so eager to work in Latin America. I also applied for an AIESEC internship in Argentina, Colombia, or Brazil.

In late April, I received a letter from J. Fulton Sears III, who acknowledged my writing to the VP of Latin America, First National Bank of Boston, but he said no positions were available. I didn't hear back from Nicaragua, so wondered if maybe I'd go to Wall Street anyway. In early May, I received a phone call from the same Mr. Sears, saying, "I understand you wrote our vice president in São Paulo. He'd like us to interview you."

I barely contained my joy and agreed to an interview that Friday. Allan saw me at Uris Hall and said, "Guess what! You've been selected as AIESEC's first intern to Brazil."

Wow, I thought, *when it rains, it pours!* He mentioned that the paid internship would be at BankBoston in São Paulo. I was stunned—how could that be—as Mr. Sears had mentioned nothing in conversation. Allan said that my knowledge of Portuguese on the application had made the difference. On Thursday night, I took the train to Beantown, which was more pleasant in May than February. I was booked into the Parker House and strolled to rustic Faneuil Hall for clam chowder.

The next morning, I entered 100 Federal Street and found Mr. Sears in the International Division. He wasn't pleased but was courteous, scheduling interviews with six senior managers. I didn't disclose the AIESEC internship, instead waiting for the right moment. I tried to present a confident face to managers, mentioning my ties to Columbia's Latin American Association and to Brazil's navy. They seemed pleasant though not inquisitive, taking me to lunch atop the bank, with spectacular views of Boston Harbor.

At 4:00 p.m., Mr. Sears left me with the VP of Latin America, speaking on the phone. He nodded, looked over his glasses, and waved me to a seat. I heard him mention Buenos Aires and remembered bank operations in Argentina, Brazil, and formerly Cuba. My first impression was that he was a bit stern. I then heard him cracking jokes *en español*, so thought maybe that was his initial façade.

He thanked me for coming and asked what I thought of the Bank. I told him that I was impressed by its commitment to Latin America and would like to become a loan officer in Brazil. He demurred and asked about Columbia and my time in the navy, which he held in high regard. Then, I dropped the bombshell: "Did you know that AIESEC's chosen me to be BancoBoston's first intern in São Paulo?"

This reserved VP seemed to wobble on his chair yet regained his stately composure, replying, "Mr. Murphy, that's perfect! You can use this time to check us out, as we certainly will you. Then let's get in touch in the fall."

I left the bank in seventh heaven and arrived at Grand Central at 11:00 p.m. I caught the subway uptown until W. 110th and entered my favorite pub, the Gold Rail, in full swing. I ran into housemates, telling them the good news. They bought rounds to celebrate, Victor offering "dessert" later on. We struggled up Broadway into our living room, where Victor served special brownies, leaving us all sky high. They toasted my coming travel, repeating, "Brazeeeel," many times.

I finished exams in late May, my excitement building for my first journey to South America. Allan suggested a side trip to Andean countries, from where I could fly to São Paulo, and he could wander Incan ruins. Wanderlust supreme, this Columbia business grad had visited more countries around the world than anyone I knew.

Samy said he'd return to São Paulo during our summer vacation, or Brazil's winter, mentioning his dad had a Boston account downtown. Victor wished me well, promising to keep the closet for the fall. I bid everyone *adios*, put on my backpack, and arrived at George Washington Bridge. I put my thumb out and got a trucker's lift down I-95, detouring to Charleston. I hung out at a station for a ride to Jacksonville and then waited hours in the rain. Four Florida State students took pity and drove me to Miami International, wishing me, "*Hasta la vista.*"

Allan met at MIA Ecuadorian Air for a rough DC-8 flight over the Andes. We dodged nearby peaks and landed in Quito, staying at a downtown bed and breakfast, whose owner made eyes for me. In the morning, we shared a bus with cackling chicken to Cuenca, the land of eternal spring. I met my pen pal, Laura, and we hugged a long time. We became a hit with her large family, sharing English, Spanish, and Allan's jokes.

I hugged Laura *adios*, catching rides to Tumbez, amid the earthquake's devastation. The bus bumped along until Lima, dropping us near a classmate's home. He took us to Granja Azul, where eaters of a dozen chickens, earned a free dinner and photo on the wall. I was stuffed after one, washing it down with *pisco* sours, Peruvian style.

As buses had fallen off mountain roads, we flew to Cuzco. We landed well but took deep breaths at eighty-five hundred feet, taking the bus to Plaza de Armas. We began speaking with residents, who said, "Tell us jokes." I served as translator to Allan's jests, answered by local hoots. I reveled in my role as interlocutor. Dozens surrounded us, telling friends about two gringos making fun *en español!* Two indigenous brothers, Richar and Edwin, befriended us, recounting their city's history before Spain's conquest in 1533.

The brothers took us to Machu Picchu. We marveled at its startling beauty and summits shrouded in clouds. Atop, I viewed a river leading to the Amazon basin, admiring this Incan city in harmony with surroundings. It felt like a religious experience, giving me hope that man and nature might be one. We returned to Cuzco, mesmerized, and dined at a local *mercado*. We've stayed in touch with those hospitable brothers until the current day.

We left for Arequipa, where Allan planned to stay. With my last fifty-dollar Amex check, I negotiated a ride to La Paz. The dynamic duo split up over hugs, going our separate ways. The taxi driver was talkative yet complained about missing soccer. We passed Lake Titicaca and floating balsa rafts, and we crossed the border amid several armed guards.

"Let me do the talking," the driver said, crossing through twelve checkpoints. La Paz, one of Bolivia's two capitals, is seated in a valley, below the plateau and airport at thirteen thousand feet. The driver put us in a cheap motel owned by relatives and said, "Breathe deeply." I tried to do so but awoke early with pain in my lungs—perhaps I'd caught pneumonia? I hyperventilated but eventually fell into a shallow sleep. The driver awoke and dropped me at the airport, where I searched for Lloyds Aereo Boliviano.

On presenting my passport and Amex card, attendants informed that LAB didn't accept credit. I offered a check, but they said, "Cash only." There were no ATMs then, and Citibank wouldn't open until 10:00 a.m. As Monday's flight departed at 8:30 a.m., I wondered what to do. The next flight for São Paulo was leaving Thursday. Stressed, I asked passengers for a loan. Some were willing but without cash. I heard the Boeing 727 starting its engines and saw someone running down the corridor.

I knelt and said, "Please, sir, help me out. I need a loan until São Paulo. I promise to pay you back." He agreed and, as it turned out, was a missionary. The flight bumped over the Andes until it smoothed out over the continent's subtropical plains, toward the red earth of São Paulo, a city of over ten million people.

A sea of buildings greeted me with red-tiled roofs, and we landed at Congonhas on a clear, winter afternoon. The missionary and I cleared customs and caught a cab to BancoBoston, where I used my Amex to repay him $150 in Brazilian *cruzeiros*. I thanked him over and over, wishing him well on his mission to Brazil's Amazon.

I looked above, said a prayer, and sought Doutora Maria, the head of personnel, who wasn't there. Her assistant pleasantly served me a sugared *cafezinho* and practiced English with the new intern. Doutora Maria arrived in a flourish and seemed thrilled that her AIESEC initiative landed this MBA. She gave me the keys to the bank's apartment in the Garden District and, with a smile, sent me on my way.

I unpacked and walked up Rua Augusta, abounding with chic boutiques and smiling paulistas, who sometimes looked back. The next morning, a beaming Doutora Maria introduced me to VP Richard, to whom I'd first written. "You sure move quickly, Steve." I explained the AIESEC connection, and he seemed pleased, assigning me special projects. From June to August, I wrote reports on new stock market funds, with my Portuguese slowly improving. Brazilians proved hospitable—including Claudio, my AIESEC host— wanting to learn my story, as I did theirs in this lively metropolis.

The time in São Paulo went quickly, amid fiestas and soccer games. I screamed along with thirty-five thousand fans at a classic in Pacaembú, where Santos's Pelé matched against Rivelino of Corinthians. Though the score ended three to three, Rivelino made sensational kicks from twenty-yards out. So, I became an aficionado of Corinthians and Brazilian *futebol*.

In late August, I visited the Marvelous City, as Rio de Janeiro was known, amazed by its physical beauty, beyond that of Hong Kong. "The girl from Ipanema" walked nonchalantly, her hair ruffled by ocean breeze. I vowed to come back, returning to São Paulo for more fiestas and reluctantly bid, "Bye-bye, Brazil!"

$$* \; * \; *$$

The fall semester went quickly, as I buckled up to finish my MBA. I interviewed at Wall Street firms, like many Columbia MBAs and got an offer from Irving Trust as junior equity analyst, starting at $25,000—not bad in 1972. I returned to Boston, where VP Frank received positive reports from Brazil. He offered me a junior credit analyst position in São Paulo, starting at $16,500. He mentioned Brazil's lower cost of living and asked for a response by the end of the term. Depending on whom I talked to, I got different advice. "Go for the money," most American students said. "Go for adventure," Latino amigos suggested.

Turning Point: Go for Riches in Wall Street or Seek the Unknown in Brazil?

I walked along Battery Park and contemplated the Statue of Liberty. Up at Wall Street, the snorting bull looked angry before the New York Stock Exchange. At a deli, I overheard brokers trading tips on stocks and bonds, wondering how I'd fit in. Outside, a shoe-shine attendant looked at my shoes, imploring, "Shine, mister?"

My shoes looked battered, so I nodded yes. As fate would have it, he was from Brazil. Three years before, he'd come to New York to visit a friend but enjoyed making money and stayed. I practiced Portuguese, which came back quickly, and thanked him for the shine. Was that brief encounter a possible sign?

That night, I sought out Allan and reminisced about our South American adventure. The next morning, I handed my Brazilian report to International Business prof David. I mentioned the two job offers, and he asked, "Steve, how risk prone are you?"

"After surviving Vietnam and my recent trip, I think I've lost my fear. Doing well at Columbia has helped a lot."

He was aware of my haunting stint at HBS but continued, "If you're interested in international business, you have a great opportunity in Brazil. But do whatever you think best."

I thanked him and ran into Mexican friends, who encouraged me to follow my heart. They said that if I ever went to Mexico, "*Mi casa es su casa.*"

In the afternoon, I picked up the phone to call Uncle Frank, as some affectionately called the Bank's VP of Latin America, and accepted his offer in São Paulo. He asked when I'd be able to start. I paused and said that I'd need a couple months.

"So Steve, what do you plan to do in the interim?" he inquired.

Thinking fast on my feet, I replied, "I may visit friends in Mexico, perhaps Haiti, and even the Dominican Republic."

Uncle Frank responded, "If you see opportunities for the bank, let me know on return."

He set April 2 as my start day and wished me safe travel. The next morning, I called Irving Trust to decline its offer, and the recruiter asked where I'd be working. I confirmed that I was accepting BankBoston's offer to return to Brazil. He said, "Take care—they sometimes have revolutions down there." I thanked him, hung up, and cast my fate to *las* Americas.

December flew by, and I headed home for the holidays. I arrived upbeat, looking forward to the future—how different from HBS days. My folks took pause on my job in São Paulo but said they'd maybe visit. My mom visited me in Hawaii and seemed open-minded, saying, "Brazil's far away, but you love Latin America." I sensed that my dad, while supportive, nurtured hopes that his eldest might take over his business. Yet he did not push, for which I thank him to this day.

I returned to Columbia, convinced that my path led south of the border not south to Wall Street. I considered hitchhiking through Mexico, and friends reaffirmed invitations in Monterrey and Mexico DF. A Haitian friend said that if I came to Port-au-Prince, his mom would love to put me up. Then my Chilean pen pal, Alberto, wrote saying he'd moved to Santo Domingo and that I should stop by. The die thus cast, I finished finals with gusto, bidding *"Hasta la vista"* to Columbia Business School. I hoisted my backpack until George Washington Bridge and put out my thumb.

This time, I overnighted in the cabs of two trucks until beautiful Mobile, where I stayed with family friends. I caught a bus to the Big Easy, and a friend of a friend hosted me in his Tulane dorm. As Mardi Gras began, we sashayed down Bourbon Street and barhopped until dawn. I cheered princesses on floats and hustled doubloons thrown by Crewe's. My memory cleared on Ash Wednesday, so I left with "refugees" to the Lone Star State. Overnighting near San Antonio's Riverwalk, I caught a bus to Monterrey, Mexico's largest industrial city.

Sergio's father welcomed me into open arms as his son just returned to Columbia for his last semester. His family showed me Monterrey's prestigious Technology Institute and asked many questions about their son. Later, their youngest and I hiked up *la Silla* (the saddle) to the family's cottage and found special mushrooms of Don Juan fame.

The family embraced me warmly and put me on a bus to San Luis Potosí. There, a business man picked me up and hosted me in his fashionable estate in Guadalajara. He introduced me to his foxy "daughter" and extolled his city of eternal spring. He offered a ride through Jalisco as he and his "daughter" were going to Acapulco for conference. They dropped me at Magdalena, where I thanked him, wondering where his wife had gone.

In the town square, I exchanged stories and jokes with residents, *a la* Cuzco. As there was no inn in this village, the town butcher offered lodging in his rustic dwelling. His family of five shared a delicious soup of vegetable beef and shots of mescal, wishing *buenas noches*. Juan showed me the bench with straw, serving as bed. With a cow and *burro* as nocturnal companions, I thought about singing "Away in a Manger." Thanking Juan for his hospitality, I left on a truck of goats for Mexico's capital in the Distrito Federal.

Mexico DF was and is the largest metropolitan area in the Western Hemisphere, numbering more than twenty million *capitalinos*. The farmer left me downtown, where I called friends. I took the metro to Coyoacán, where Cortez once lived, and José Antonio remembered me as bedraggled, wearing a backpack and dirty jeans. Het graciously bid me enter his colonial home and take a long shower. I thanked him profusely and immediately fell into restful sleep.

We visited Chapultepec Park, where Mexican families took leisurely strolls and vendors sold watermelon with chili a la mode. Appreciating their graciousness, I thanked them but hit the road again. I hitched a ride to Campeche on another truck, sleeping overnight with workers. We arrived Oaxaca, in time for local festivities.

As I was born in March, Piscis Lodge caught my attention. There I met Dorita, a lady of independent spirit, who cooked vegetarian meals when natural foods were hard to find. Ahead of her time, she hosted a program on Oaxaca's public TV, called *Good & Cheap*, encouraging families to serve healthy but affordable meals. Oaxacan cuisine at Dora's table was always exquisite, topped by several chili peppers to add cha, cha, cha! Her son and I enjoyed chats with visitors from around the world, drawn to Dora's special place.

We stood arm-in-arm at the station. I boarded a bus to Mérida in Yucatán and, on arrival, walked toward the fishing village, Progreso. On the beach, I spent the night under the docks with street kids who said I was the first gringo to share their beach. I used my pack as a pillow and fell off to sleep. Late morning, I walked with the head teen, visiting his friend on a shrimp boat. He secured a grouper and roasted it over a campfire with Dora's chili peppers thrown in.

The teen said his friend's boat was heading to Jamaica on a special errand and might take me as crew. Could I pay the captain fifty dollars and him a finder's fee? Agreed, if they took me to Kingston to use my Amex again. We shook hands over my last Mexican *pesos*, and I left late afternoon on this forty-foot trawler, waving adios to teens on the loose.

Captain Samuel was short and gruff, so I usually stayed out of his way. We put out homemade nets hung from old bike tires, using fish guts as bait. We waited until sundown—which came fast in the tropics—and saw shrimp eyes glow eerily in the dark. We pulled in our catch, putting it on ice, and headed northeast toward Kingston Bay. We made good time through modest seas, overnighting twice, until dawn on the third day.

The captain docked among trawlers, taking us ashore. We had coffee outside Barclay's, watching downtown Kingston wake up. The town had a shabby feel, maybe unsafe at night. Captain Sam packed a fishing knife, guarding his package and gringo. Bank doors opened and I presented my Amex to withdraw $150. The teller called her Anglo manager, who looked over his glasses and asked for my passport. I gave it, saying I was on holiday, before beginning my job at BankBoston. He brightened at the bank's mention, nodded to the teller and said, "Welcome to Jamaica." Captain Sam received fifty dollars and nodded. I repaired to the bathroom, hiding a hundred dollars in my shoe.

The manager pointed me toward the station, advising that the North Shore would be more to my liking. I bought a ticket to Montego Bay and boarded the twelve-thirty bus with hippie tourists and talkative Jamaicans.

En route, I chatted with a local, asking her about less touristic places to visit. She looked me over and said, "Robin's Bay for you." After a three-hour, bumpy ride, she pointed to the Shell station, saying, "There you go, my lad. Follow the road till its end, and Robin's Bay 'twill be."

I thanked her and stepped off the bus, following another road less travelled. After an hour, the road faded into a path, where two people nodded, looking surprised but moving on. I passed banana trees, bougainvillea, and chattering parakeets. Night fell, and the trail ended at a blockhouse that had music coming from within.

I entered a small room with men and women dancing to Bob Marley tunes. They looked amused at me but continued on. The bartender smiled, and I was thirsty. He gave me something to drink. I was hungry, and he gave me something to eat. I didn't have shelter, so he called, "Herbert, a visitor's arrived. Come hither."

A tall, thin Jamaican nodded and asked, "Are you American?" I said yes, and he said, "Give me a quarter," which I did.

He led me outside, speaking with friends in a circle. He received a five-inch stogie, lit up, and smoked in deliberate manner, passing it on. I took a quick hit, yet he asked, "What's the hurry, *mon*?" Since I hardly smoked—occasionally eating Victor's brownies—I quickly elevated and felt I was heading to Mars. Herbert and friends spoke in incomprehensible Creole, smiling a lot. He led me away through sugar cane fields higher than we were. It dawned on me that here was whitey in a black country, where race relations hadn't been good, in the middle of nowhere.

Yet onward I went—my fear left somewhere behind. We arrived at a wooden shack under a tin roof, with two kids and a dog sleeping in the doorstep. Herbert opened the curtain, saying, "Woman, get thee from thy bed—the visitor is here!" I tried to beg off as I had a sleeping bag, yet he insisted, "Tonight you sleep in my bed." So I did.

I didn't remember anything untoward on that narrow bed, except that he snored a lot. I eventually fell asleep and was awakened when his wife entered to prepare breakfast. She feigned indifference as we slept. We eventually gathered outside, eating a delicious breakfast of ackee and saltfish, plantains, and rice. Later, we walked uphill to "work" in his taro patch, Herbert greeting neighbors and showing off his American visitor.

He introduced me to his younger sister with whom I spent time. She had a sparkle in her eye and enjoyed watching me swim nude in azure waters sheltered by Robin's Bay. I pinched myself to ask if this might be paradise, staying two more days. Yet leave I should to arrive in Haiti where others awaited.

So with a heavy heart, I bid Herbert and his family good-bye: "Herbert, thank you for your wonderful generosity, but I have to leave to catch a plane."

He looked shocked, saying, "What's the hurry, *mon*? You have your home here. My sister's here. You have our love. What more you want, *mon*?"

I teared up without words to say. How could I match his gracious spirit, given to this visitor from afar? Sadly and looking back, I saw them vanish behind cane fields as I walked up the narrow road to the Shell station, wondering if I'd lived a dream. I took another bus into Kingston and the flight to Port-au-Prince, yet Herbert's words haunted me throughout my journey.

In Port-au-Prince, I took a jitney and, in French, asked my way to Ruelle Roi, the residence of Madame Rock. Her son had written, and she gave me a long hug, not releasing my hand. She introduced me to her light-skinned daughter and two younger children. I freshened up and toured the neighborhood, her daughter guiding me to the Olafson Hotel. The site of Graham Greene's novel, *The Comedians*, we saw its maître d' sharing gossip and Baby Doc speeding off. We smiled and enjoyed the tropical breeze.

The next day, I pressed my corduroy coat, which lay at the bottom of my pack. I walked downtown to visit La Banque Central d'Haiti—what did I have to lose? I arrived midmorning and asked to speak with its president, Monsieur André, in behalf of the First National Bank of Boston. His assistant served me coffee in demitasse and brought me into a large room. She presented me to a balding man, a subtle smile on his lips. We spent an hour talking about our different cities and family lives. He then said that the Bank wouldn't need any capital to set up a branch. I replied that should please our VP, wishing him *merci* and a smile for her.

I considered crossing the border by bus, but Madame Rock said "*Non, Etienne*, better a plane." She and her family gave more long hugs and took me to the airport. I left in the late afternoon, crossing the mountains to the greener side of Hispaniola. Despite an electrical storm, we landed at Santo Domingo's airport.

Alberto waited outside with a chauffeured car, furnished by Falconbridge, where he worked as controller. We'd corresponded for years, and he'd stayed with Aunt Maxine, graduating from Portland University. He was from a traditional family in Santiago, Chile, but had worked for multinationals abroad. His wife and children enjoyed their time in the Dominican Republic but had challenges, as did I, understanding Dominican accents, trading *r* for *l* sounds in spoken words.

To accomplish my mission, I donned my sport coat and borrowed a tie to meet the president of El Banco Central de la Republica Dominicana. I had a longer wait in the lobby but eventually entered an elegant room. The president sat behind his desk with three advisors seated around. I introduced myself in behalf of the bank, saying this was my first time to their beautiful country.

They appreciated my compliment and began to tell me about their lives in Santo Domingo, eventually getting down to business. They advised that rules prohibited foreign banks opening a branch in the Dominican Republic, unlike in Haiti. However, they said joint ventures were permitted, if partners were local. "Do you know such groups?" I inquired. They replied that they did, smiling, for even members of their families were in these groups. I thanked them for their time and information, feeling an accomplished emissary for the bank.

Alberto's family congratulated me over a special dinner at La Romana and then took me to the airport for my flight to New York City. We embraced—and have maintained—our friendship over decades, our families visiting wherever our paths might meet.

Caribbean memories lulled me to sleep, dreaming of paradise in Robin's Bay. How blessed I felt by meeting people like Herbert, Merida's beach kids, and so many other kind people during my odyssey! I gave thanks again to a greater power watching over me.

Yet, another phase in life lay ahead. So I pressed my suit and straightened my tie, readying myself as a young professional for my first day on the job.

CHAPTER 4

Rival Cities: São Paulo and Rio

THE DAY AFTER April Fools' Day, I entered the pregnant-looking building on Federal Street, headquarters of the First National Bank of Boston. After finishing up with HR, I stopped by Uncle Frank's office. When I got there, he said, "Let's get out of here!" He took me to the same chowder house at Faneuil Hall and asked about my trip. I offered an edited version, highlighting visits with central bank presidents of Haiti and Dominican Republic. I confessed hitching rides through Mexico and a shrimp boat to Jamaica, to which he said, "You'd have liked Cuba in the good ole days." As the former general manager in Havana, he had a reputation for lively fiestas and had married a delightful Cuban lady.

He tasked me to write a report to open a branch in Haiti and a joint venture in the Dominican Republic, as well as to begin credit training. For three months, I became immersed in cash and fund flow analyses as well as with asset and liability ratios to ascertain the good, bad, or ugly in credit. "Of course," Chief Credit Officer Lin said, "if it doesn't feel right, just walk away." Upper management approved my proposals for Port-au-Prince and Santo Domingo, making this junior officer proud.

I said my good-byes to Uncle Frank and international personnel, catching Pan Am in tourist class, as the bank didn't upgrade. An electrical storm over the Amazon shook me awake. Later, Brasilia came into view—its urban contour shaped like a plane. We arrived at Viracopos Airport, early on July 9, a holiday only in São Paulo, commemorating the rebellion against Brazil's federal government in 1932. *Paulistas* didn't cotton to the feds, especially if lodged in Rio, so they revolted, celebrating ever since.

The bank reserved its trendy Garden District apartment, the watchman remembering and welcoming me "home." I soon walked Rua Augusta, where young men revved engines and cruised up and down. They honked, calling to girls who pretended not to notice while window-shopping. If a young macho proved successful in securing conversation or a phone number, he'd become the man among peers. So I walked through this human carnival, catching glances on its streets.

The bank downtown had the appearance of a wedding cake, layering toward the top, offering "colonial dining" to special clients. I greeted Doutora Maria, who welcomed me effusively with hugs, kisses, and cafezinho. She mentioned the new VP of Brazil came from Argentina, as her favorite, Sr. Richard, had accepted an offer outside. I'd been assigned work with an Anglo-Argentine in pension and stock funds.

The early months included some credit analysis and more outreach to Brazilian partners. I'd lunch with Boston fund managers, often mediating gaucho-Julio brags about prize bulls versus Colorado Joe's American buffalo. Afterward, we'd walk the narrow streets around São Paulo's stock exchange, admiring attractive passersby. After work, I'd grab Brazilian *chopps* beer with colleagues, relishing this way of life.

Next, I found a row apartment above a key shop, paying $200 monthly, transforming it into another bachelor pad, including a red-room cushion covering the floor. I threw lively fiestas, inviting colleagues and friends of friends—a key relationship in Brazil. Samy returned and took me on blind dates at his club. As the bank allowed expats to join one social club, he recommended Clube Paulistano, featuring pools and tennis for São Paulo's well to do.

Brazilians had song in their lives. Popular music told of loves imagined and loves foregone, registering deep marks on the Brazilian psyche. Songwriters wrote music of double entendre, subtly advocating freedom, annoying Brazil's military rulers in 1972. It was a tough balancing act, but musicians prevailed over military censors, which were slow on the uptake. At parties, we strummed guitars or percussion and sang along. At concerts, we danced in the aisles, energizing the band.

"Living life to the fullest," became my mantra, both at social functions or while walking the streets. I cheered on Corinthians soccer with gusto and danced with casual partners after midnight. I came home at dawn, hearing bells calling the faithful to Mass. But this young professional didn't rise on Sunday mornings—instead I did later for lunch or afternoon play.

After a year, the new VP called me in, saying he'd observed my progress but wanted my talents elsewhere. "How'd you like to become our international officer in Rio?" he asked. I was surprised, appreciating his offer—when did he need to know? "Next Monday," he intoned. I kibitzed with friends like James, with whom I'd shared beer. He observed that loan officers had more defined career paths. At the club, I encountered Samy, who said he'd miss Saturday escapades and trips to São Paulo's coast. He thought the job a step upward—and in the Marvelous City. So why not?

I accepted the VP of Brazil's offer and checked with Doutora Maria on logistics. The next month went quickly with good-bye parties at homes, clubs, and the red room. I sold the little I had to the key man below, who coveted my red mattress. James offered chopps at Cantina Piolin, saying, "I may see you in Rio, sooner than you think."

In Rio, a friend suggested staying in a group apartment in Copacabana's Posto 5, named for Petrobras fifth station along Copa's famous beach. Chico said that the group was eclectic, with an attitude of live and let live. He, like Victor in New York City, enjoyed spicing up tropical brownies, and I didn't complain. The apartment was close to the beach, so I swam often to escape Rio's heat.

The old branch was near Rio's port, a transitional district, transforming to tawdry by night. The bank had originally financed coffee exports but was relocating closer to Chase and Citibank. During Rio's popular Carnaval, however, the Avenue assumed a different personality but on most days streamed with cars toward Guanabara Bay. Sidewalks became pedestrian thoroughfares, coursing with bankers and office boys and girls, often looking back for better views. A gringo by appearance, I stayed vigilant for pickpockets while navigating streets or buses.

Resident VP, Bob, known as a *simpatico* storyteller and golfer, greeted me warmly. He looked forward to another American to participate in Rio's American Society and Chamber, representing ten thousand compatriots. He wished me well in securing international loans and, looking down, said the new manager came from Buenos Aires.

The Argentine manager's jaw was taut, as he tasked me to visit international companies as soon as possible. "With pleasure," I said, seeing smirks on loan officers' faces. Brazilians and Argentines traditionally didn't mix—especially at soccer matches. Brazilians didn't appreciate Argentine airs of superiority or being called lazy—even "monkeys." The Argentine accent sounded harsh to Brazil's flowing Portuguese, creating tense social scenes. Yet the bank had appointed him as Rio's manager, so this new kid on the block had to make the best of it—and did.

I was assigned to prospect Brazilian exporters and foreign multinationals. My favorite was Bacardi Rum's subsidiary nearby. I met its hard charging manager from Miami and its soft-spoken CFO, speaking about our families, the Bacardis, and *futebol*. The CEO adjourned, saying they'd consider our proposal over lunch. We all had *caipirissimas*, a version of Brazil's national drink, made from light rum, lime juice, and sugar, mixed over ice—or tropical limeade with a punch.

"We like your manner," the CEO said, agreeing to the export line. "You'll be our man." I left lunch on a high. Telling the manager, I received a raised eyebrow and request to present to the committee. I marshaled data on Bacardi's growing, international brand and secured credit approval with one dissenting vote.

VP Bob said, "Good work, Steve! Come by my home—let's celebrate!" I took the hot bus to Copacabana to shower and change into casual wear. In banks, loan officers wore a coat and tie, ending the day in deep sweat. A shower after work provided me a transition to festivities at night. I walked along Copacabana toward Ipanema, reaching Bob's apartment. The doorman called upstairs, ushering me to Bob's ornate penthouse. The view was extraordinary, as waves broke on Ipanema's beach and kids played soccer under lights. The breeze rose after sunset, refreshing us after Rio's heat.

Bob offered me *caipirinha* and scotch for himself, and we chatted over a three-course dinner, including shrimp *muqueca*. He said, "We love Rio's laid-back lifestyle. It's so different from São Paulo. You'll have to loosen up here. *Cariocas*, as Rio's residents are called, don't like hard asses. But you're a bachelor—so no big deal

"Any other advice as I sort things out?" I inquired.

"Yes, don't take things at face value—look beyond their words," Bob continued, looking at his boys. "We go back to the States, once a year, and that's fine by us."

Later, my parents called, saying they'd join a trade mission to Brazil to import rosewood tables and chairs. When they arrived, we walked along Copacabana, enjoying exotic scenes like beach volleyball, thinly clad bathers, and kites plying the sky. My dad and I enjoyed the views and the time together. When asked where I lived, I pointed briefly to our group apartment but changed conversation to my international career. I proudly showed them Rio under the tropical sun, so different from Seattle, where rains kept coming down. We hugged, and I took them to their plane for São Paulo, and later back home.

My days began early—jogging, swimming, and having fresh orange juice. I'd take the cool bus downtown, arriving at 9:30 a.m. to visit clients during the day. A business lunch was a treat, but credit presentations were not so. I left after 7:00 p.m., having beer at nearby Casa Simpatia, returning home for my night out and about. I'd eventually hear the warning by the apartment's owner, unhappy about nocturnal visitors.

December arrived with temperatures reaching forty degrees Celsius (104° F). Cariocas, named after Disney's parrot character, believed government authorities misled about official temperatures, keeping them lower than reality. Forty degrees Celsius seemed like a psychological turning point, as cariocas worked slowly, dreaming of chopps or adventures at night. Productivity plummeted, though air-conditioning mitigated summer's heat—until we went outside again.

One Sunday, I traveled to the North Zone, away from the beach. Rio, shaped like a *J*, has the hook of the *J* in the South Zone, with Copacabana and Ipanema beaches, and the stem in the North, where most residents live, beyond tourists' eyes. A colleague invited me to lunch, but I'd left the address home. Deciding to look around the Tijuca neighborhood, I spied a favela beyond. I entered a paved street, which soon turned into cobblestones, winding up a hill called Salgueiro. I received surprised looks and calls from youngsters, unused to gringo visits. I kept climbing as cobblestones turned into dirt road, recalling my trek to Robin's Bay. Above, I heard samba playing and confronted six guys, who raised their chins, asking, "*Que passa?*"

"I'd heard samba above and was going there," I answered, wondering what'd come next.

A dark-skinned youth, acting as leader, pointed his fingers to his head like a pistol, saying, "Bang, bang—dangerous, gringo!"

Another, called Buddha, proposed, "Bring me a bottle of whiskey on Sunday, blondie, and I'll show you samba of the hills."

"With pleasure," I answered, following him down. I met his parents, Severina and Moacyr, and promised to return. My adventurous side won that round, though my heart beat pretty loud.

The next week, business wound down as cariocas planned for holiday fiestas. Clients often gave gifts, such as Christmas baskets, to loan officers. As Bacardi's officer, I received twelve-year *añejo* rum and hoped to celebrate. But not so fast, as the apartment's owner said, "You're all out by month's end!"

With that concern, I returned to Salgueiro and found his parents playing canasta. I joined them and chatted about families, samba, and heat.

They called me "Estive," putting a vowel before the consonant, like most Brazilians do. Later, Severina served her delicious black beans and rice, whose aroma brought in sons and grandchildren from the street. Jorge, a.k.a., Buddha, appeared with his brothers, adding my whiskey to his drink. They asked where I was staying, so I said, "Temporarily in this group house in Copacabana, though we'll all have to leave by the end of the month"

Severina looked at husband, who nodded. She replied, "Estive, you can stay with us! Jorge has a trundle under his bed—you're welcome here as our American son."

I choked up at her spontaneous invitation. How could I refuse generosity from this mother of the hill? So I said, "*Obrigado*," or obliged, and yes, as their American son. They asked questions about America, snow, and Santa Claus—hard to imagine in tropical heat. I learned that Buddha's brothers had other families around, dividing time with their parents and others up the hill.

At midnight, we caught a ride to their samba school, entering a courtyard with hundreds dancing to tambourines. I recalled the Brazilian ship's band, when musicians never stopped playing, coming and going from the bandstand. Buddha spiked beer with whiskey—especially if conversations dragged. His brothers joked about rival soccer teams, provoking voices to erupt. Insults followed with laughter.

Some ladies took pity on this gringo's hips, shaking them softly to improve my beat. After a fashion, I got into the swing, receiving smiles and phone numbers as reward. I bid my new brothers *ciao*, and negotiated fare for Copacabana, encountering the group house in wild affair.

On Christmas Eve, I told Chico of the invite from this family on the hill. "You're an adventurer," he said, "fond of living on the edge." We attended midnight Mass and returned home, not having a family dinner to attend. His family in São Paulo was traveling, and mine was far away. Most families celebrated Christmas dinner in the early morning, all generations taking part. As diners said *ciao* with hugs and air kisses, the youngest awaited Christmas day, hitting the beach. I said my own good-bye to Copacabana with a jog through surf toward Sugar Loaf, returning to catch the hot bus to Rio's North Zone.

My Salgueiro family overflowed with hospitality, mending any inconvenience. Besides Estive, they called me Russian or "blondie" for my light complexion. Its residents became aware of the *americano* among them, protected by family hospitality. I'd wander the hills without fear, enjoying celebrity status but being a good neighbor.

Except one evening. A *policia militar* (PM) van arrived abruptly, slamming on its brakes. We stopped and wondered what was going on, as fear and disgust ruled emotions toward the military police. Apparently, a PM had issues with a lady of the night, roughing her up. I asked what was happening.

"What's it to you?" He pushed me to the ground, asking for my ID. I gave my journalist card as the *Brazil Herald's* stringer. Under the military, everyone was required to carry government ID, which I'd left at home.

"*Babaca*," or "fool," he called me, circling with five others, toting guns.

"Get lost, or get in trouble, gringo," he commanded, as I staggered off the cobblestones. My brothers nodded sadly, realizing that their family's protection didn't extend to PMs on their hill.

New Year's Eve arrived with samba and Roman candles. Most everyone knew their neighbors, so the fiesta was like a big family reunion—aunts danced with nephews, girls danced with girls or boyfriends, and fathers danced with daughters or friends of friends. The *mulata* of my first encounter shook my hips again, coaxing out a samba rhythm. I didn't protest, continuing on until morning's light.

My daily routine changed in Salgueiro—the beaches were far away. I'd queue for the bathroom and sit down to cafezinho, enjoying the baker's warm bread. We'd say *ciao* to our parents, walking down to catch hot buses to different directions. I wore long-sleeve shirts, donning a tie in the WC. Wiping down sweat with deodorant, I'd put on my public face for Banco de Boston. Behind my desk, I'd keep a sports jacket for arrival.

January began slowly. I kept visiting Brazilian exporters, pitching dollar loans. At the branch, a new team joined us, headed by Larry, making longer-term dollar loans to firms, like Petrobras and Vale. They sold off or syndicated tranches to international banks, seeking Brazilian exposure. BankBoston, as syndicator, made commissions for arranging the loan and a slice of interest paid by Brazilian borrowers.

I justified such loans to clients, needing long-term funds for expansion, which were unavailable in local currency. However, dollar loans were not for the faint of heart, as borrowers essentially bet that they'd earn more in cruzeiros than they'd pay abroad in dollars. This bet served them well in the seventies but not the eighties when Brazil suffered major currency devaluations. For banks making dollar loans, it was the best of times, funding Brazil's economic miracle.

While loans boosted Brazil's economy, every family had to make ends meet. Each member contributed to family income, including brothers and adopted sons. We brought part of our salary every two weeks to Severina, who controlled the purse strings. She'd often trade tomatoes in her garden for a neighbor's squash or exchange work favors. We all helped keep our family afloat.

As Carnaval got closer, drummers beat intently, and dancers choreographed new steps. We decorated floats and readied costumes, while celebrities paid high sums to affiliate. Our pageant retold stories of escaping slaves and refugee rulers in Brazil's northeast. Costumes, songs, and dances reflected that theme. As Salgueiro's drummers were considered Rio's best, expectations ran sky high that year.

Behind every school, however, lurked someone from the animal game or local numbers racket. Cariocas would choose a four-number series, each representing an animal, such as an alligator or lion, from local bookies. Winning series were based on the national lottery's drawing, and bookies always paid up. Dealers controlled street corners, transacting citywide. Big wigs had defined turf and didn't encroach on another's without severe consequence. The animal man funded his favorite samba school, fronting initial costs. The winning school would compensate the bigwig, earning prestige, invitations, and gratuities around the world.

Buddha asked if I'd like to "go down the Avenue" with Salgueiro's percussion. I was flattered, but said that my American rhythm might traverse their samba. Buddha said not to worry. I'd play the *chocalho*, a homemade instrument with small pebbles inside, sounding like "shoo, shoo" when shaken. It was the least among instruments but provided subtle touches to beating drums. How could I say no? So I said yes and, with limited skills, practiced nonstop.

Bob learned that I was going out with the samba school, congratulating me: "You'll be the first banker to dance down the avenue." The manager frowned but said nothing, as I continued expanding Rio's international business.

Brazil received more favorable reviews from international publications, despite critiques from the *New York Times*. Under General Geisel, repression was lighter, but rumblings continued of artists missing if they didn't toe the line. However, cariocas felt more prosperous as Carnaval approached, just in time.

Carnaval, spelled in Brazil with an *a,* is like Mardi Gras, which from medieval times, was known for wild commemorations of pleasure preceding Ash Wednesday's Lent. Brazil, colonized by the Portuguese, took this popular festival to another dimension. I was excited to take part in what was called the "Greatest Show on Earth," playing my *chocalho.* Carnaval officially began Saturday with club parties, followed Sunday and Monday by samba schools down the Avenue. Tuesday was the last hurrah, spent in discos or hot bedrooms. Brazilians celebrated nationwide, though not much in São Paulo, whose residents escaped to Bahia or interior cities. Yet in Rio, Carnaval reached apotheosis along its streets.

Over the years, I've concluded that Brazilian personal calendars began and ended in *Carnaval*—especially relationships. At the time, I was lightly dating the *mulata* who'd slipped me her number at Salgueiro. She enjoyed presenting me as her gringo, yet I'd heard of her other "friend" around. I didn't cotton becoming a show horse to her family and acquaintances, so I became restless for new encounters. Meanwhile, temperatures broke forty degrees Celsius, as lust and samba rose high in Rio's North Zone.

Saturday was muggy, with residents slowly rising. Salgueiro and five others were slated to perform on Sunday night, with the remaining schools Monday—all seeking the grand prize. I tried on my white costume with red trim, joining brothers in practice. At sunset, we heard of spies from the rival Mangueira penetrating headquarters but being chased off by guards. Carnaval was serious business. Its school allegory and rhythm were confidential indeed.

Sunday arrived beneath humid heat—our samba reaching feverous pitch. We practiced but adjourned quickly as tropical rain chased us down the hill. I ran and slipped but found shelter at Almir's abode. Later, we took in another band member, whose shack had washed away. We then readied ourselves for the big event, hurrying to rendezvous at Rio's train station, Central do Brasil.

We waited outside, drinking chopps and observing our rival parade down the Avenue. Under light rain, we found our section for this choreographed event, adjusting costumes and tambourines. The band preceded the singers and dancers on the floats, providing rhythm. We moved into place at 1:30 a.m., following Mangueira in its wake.

Fans paying high prices cheered us from the bleachers, including jetsetters like Mick Jagger. Others penetrated police cordons to grab peeks between the seats. I caught glimpses of *mulatas*, smiling, twirling, and exuding heat. We sashayed by Salgueiro's "throne," its president holding court with foreign visitors and transvestite queens. On we drummed, turning at Avenida Rio Branco, into human waves, flowing to our catatonic beat.

Wafting above, I heard my name and nodded proudly to colleagues dancing in the streets. Another "Estive" rung out from an actress in plumes, waving with red-faced gringos hanging on. The crowd swayed to our theme, two-stepping with passersby. At the Museum of Beaux Arts, revelers overflowed windows, showering us in confetti. Finally, I reached the Avenue's end, in time to catch my breath.

On The Edge

We slowed at Praça do Paris, joining schools in quiet retreat. We continued playing samba and followed friends to parties upstairs in Lapa. On the balcony, I swayed to another rhythm played by strangers of the night.

Monday was our day of rest. We saw TV Globo's reviews of Salgueiro's steady beat and watched schools parade where we'd once been. We admired Mocidade's drummers, known for their expertise.

On Tuesday, we returned to our dance hall, offering around-the-clock samba. I sighed my last hurrah of Carnaval, squinting awkwardly in morning light.

On Ash Wednesday, banks opened after noon. I arrived late and was greeted as a hero by bank employees. We chatted about Carnaval, including about lovers won or lost. A light day of "work," we nursed headaches and slowed our pace.

That year, Salgueiro won the grand prize, edging Mocidade on our drummer's beat. Mangueira finished third. Our residents erupted in joy: "We won Carnaval!" In costume, we danced down the hill to our neighborhood's acclaim!

As summer's heat faded, life returned to a normal rhythm. I added export business, gaining branch prestige, and travelled to Salvador, Recife, and Fortaleza. Salvador of Bahia was Brazil's first capital, where slaves disembarked. With Afro-Brazilian roots, Bahia held mystique, serving as a spiritual center. There, Candomblé vied for souls among Catholic saints and would draw me back another day.

Returning with business, I thought Bob would be encouraging, but I saw concern written on his face. Someone had complained to São Paulo about my living in the hills, presenting an improper image of the bank. That news cut wind from my sails and raised my temper.

But Bob, a friend and ally, said, "Steve, just think about it." I counted to ten to keep my anger in check, giving the Argentine manager a hard look on the way out.

* * *

Aware of my plight, a colleague invited me to view an upstairs apartment, or *sobrado*, on a hill in Copacabana's Posto 4. The charming colonial apartment was for sale by its original owner, with a balcony, garage, and avocado tree. I closed the deal on the spot—some in dollars to the seller's account offshore and the balance in Brazilian cruzeiros, financed by a bank. Sellers often lowered a price to avoid the stamp tax, preferring dollars off the books. My cruzeiro loan paid 6 percent per annum, plus monetary correction, added to my loan balance, to compensate inflation's effect, running then at 30 percent p.a.

My family was sad about my moving to the South Zone, with its beaches and boutiques, but somehow understood. I said that my home was always open. Yet the look in their eyes reminded me of Herbert's in Robin's Bay. They visited my new apartment incline toward the Hill of the Goats. They nodded approval and offered Salgueiro's band to warm it up: I accepted with glee! Our families continue staying in touch, while Severina and Moacyr now smile down from heaven.

Local artisans recreated the room of passion in my new apartment. I began holding monthly parties, inviting cariocas of all shades and persuasions. Salgueiro friends often provided a samba beat, and visitors helped shake the red spread from my windows, providing light relief in Rio's heat.

My work continued to please Bob, if not the other, but some equilibrium was reached. To out of town firemen, I often served as a tour guide. When Uncle Frank visited, we adjourned to a beachside café. He asked how I was settling in. I described my life at Salgueiro and new pad in Copacabana, of which he was aware. He asked how I was faring with cariocas. To which I replied, "I sometimes get confused by words '*eu te amo.*' With another partner, might not similar words of love be offered? I wonder where I stand."

"Steve, maybe she loved you at that moment and perhaps someone else another day."

"Hmmm," I said in frustration, "so how do I figure out Brazilian character?"

"Brazilians are like the Japanese. The words aren't important. Rather, the context in which they're said." He spoke about the importance of body language and of broaching issues elliptically not frontally, like Americans tended to do.

He mentioned Drummond de Andrade, poet laureate of Brazil, paraphrasing "The Shame of Being Brazilian": "How can a foreigner understand us, if we say yes but really mean no, and when we say no, we mean maybe, and if we ever say maybe, we truly mean never?"

Maybe that was part of my problem—I should read more carefully in between the lines. I thanked Uncle Frank for his words to the wise. I began pondering my own one-night stands, wondering if I were confident enough to venture beyond casual liaisons.

Michael, a Ford Foundation friend, introduced me to an Afro-Brazilian star in TV Globo *novellas* and motion picture, *Xica da Silva*. Zezé was serving Brazil's national dish, initiated centuries before by slaves in northeastern plantations. Apparently, slaves took the remains of their master's pork roast, added beans, garlic, and spices, and served it over rice and collard greens. The masters liked this tasty dish and brought it inside the manor. Brazil has since celebrated *feijoada* every Saturday afternoon.

Zezé welcomed me among twenty guests of all colors of Brazil. Her TV Globo colleague arrived late with a stunning Afro-Brazilian actress, named Graça. She had a broad smile and fine features, and she showered me with attention. She came from Minas but was keen to know the States. Graça hadn't heard of Seattle but dreamed about Hollywood and New York City. I mentioned my stint in the Big Apple, seeing her eyes sparkle brightly. Over *caipirinhas, feijoada*, and laughter, we began a romance that languid afternoon.

Socially, we stood out at soirees—she was an Afro-Brazilian beauty with this Anglo *americano*. We enjoyed each other's company, without placing demands, appearing on society pages and photo studio prints. Graça made waves in her popular soap opera, attending parties at my *sobrado* with glitterati of all hues. Socially and professionally on the move, I felt I had landed on top of the world. Yet somehow word filtered to the head office that "Murphy might be going native," raising questions anew.

* * *

As spring turned again to summer, I returned to Casa Simpatia on a muggy night. I ordered chopps and agreed to a youngster's request to shine my shoes. His name was Beto.

"Many shines, Beto?" I inquired.

"No, you're the first—maybe you'll bring luck," he said, glancing around.

"I haven't seen you before—do you come often?"

"No, I usually work at o Central, but the watchman chased me off. Now, I'm on the edge." He glared and said, "Life's a shit."

"Life's not easy, Beto, but not always a shit," I replied, trying to give a ray of hope.

"No, life's a shit," he said with determination. "Every time I think it's getting better, life screws me again. Maybe I'll win the animal game." He pounded harder on my shoes.

"But can't you go home to escape the streets?"

"My home is anywhere, *americano*," he slurred. "My family is no more. I'm a captain of the streets."

An older boy arrived, greeting Beto: "How're things, little brother?"

"More or less, my comrade. Only one pair of shoes tonight. Life's a shit."

His friend asked me, "Are you from New York, Meester?"

"No, I'm from Seattle, where Boeing jets are made," I said.

"Zoom," he mimicked, swooping his arms and hugging Beto. "My brother shines shoes so well!" He got up and asked other patrons for a shine, as a crippled boy arrived with his hunchback mother crying out for alms.

I gave them pocket change, as Beto looked curiously at me. Back and forth flew his rag to a rhythm of the streets—until it fell slack again. I followed his gaze to two kids his age, kicking a papier-mâché soccer ball.

A goal was scored and both ran to a lady who gave each a hug. Beto gazed intensely, stopping his shoeshine samba, so I said, "*Que passa*, Beto?"

"Nothing," he said halfheartedly, bowing his head over my shoes. His eyes glistening. He said, "I watched them play. They ran to her for hugs. You see, *americano*, I never knew my mother. I don't know a mother's embrace."

No longer could I swallow beer or pizza, which arrived beneath his hungry eyes. Without words, I pushed cruzeiros into hands of the surprised waiter and shoeshine boy, who said, "Thanks, Meester, but are you OK?"

"I'm not feeling well, Beto—help yourself to the pizza with your friend."

"I know, Meester. Life's a shit," he said, adding, "but maybe it'll get better?"

I caught a cab before the first drops of rain and saw Beto sitting on his box, looking at the mother with her kids. He glanced briefly at me, grabbed some pizza, and started whistling "Jingle Bells" to his bossa nova beat.

That third week of December, we held a party for Beto and fifty other kids at my Copacabana apartment: Can you spot him on this book cover, holding the balloon?

Thanks to colleagues and clients, kids celebrated in style—Peter of McDonalds brought sandwiches; Julio, kid's clothes; Bruno Caloi, a new bicycle; and Gabriel Habib, many toys. We found youngsters on beaches and side streets, arriving at my apartment on the hill. We celebrated Christmas with Santa Claus, bedecked in red, handing presents to everyone. Thus began our Christmas tradition for Rio's street captains. Perhaps a drop in the bucket, yes. Yet we offered one day of happiness for shoeshine boys and bankers together when life was not a "shit."

Lesson from Rio's streets: When passing someone in humble state, I'll greet with a nod or smile. If the person is hungry, I'll buy something to eat. If he or she is broke, I'll offer change. If someone is needier, I'll try to do more.

After New Year, headquarters suggested a position in its Miami International office. The job would solicit well-to-do clients for personal, not corporate, services. I visited Miami and sensed a place without verve—retirees on the beach. Meeting with Boston's powers that be, I argued my experience was in corporate banking, thus not their ideal candidate. They reluctantly agreed and sent me back to Rio for another year.

A silver lining appeared when a deft carioca named Armando became acting manager, displacing the Argentine. He appointed me head of Rio's team of ten officers, loosening our leash. Our team grew branch portfolio rapidly, surpassing São Paulo, despite Rio's smaller size. We also increased exposure to infrastructure projects, such as Ludwig's reforestation in Brazil's Amazon and cashew farmers in its Northeast. As inflation increased, so too did cruzeiro interest rates, reaching a high of 63 percent p.a. We finally moved to our new building with *Jornal do Brasil*, in the heart of Rio's financial district.

Socially, I was seeing Graça and others from time to time and Salgueiro friends at monthly fiestas. Another friend, Juvenal, tried teaching me *capoeira*, Brazil's marshal art, but my gringo moves were out of sync. Instead, I took up my flute again and played bossa nova tunes with him on the *berimbau*. I also began writing *Twelve Hidden Portraits*, recounting public and private lives of Rio's residents and scored an agent in New York City. I had trouble finishing this novel while working at the bank, my analytical overpowering my creative brain. Unfortunately on my next move stateside, I lost the manuscript.

As the year wore on, headquarters inquired of my next professional move. Up-and-coming Senior VP Chad was establishing a new multinational division, marketing bank services to *Fortune* 500 companies around the world. He recruited senior domestic and international officers and visited Rio with his pitch: Would I join him as the Latin America officer for his new start-up?

Turning Point: Return to Headquarters for Professional Advancement or Stay an Expatriate in Rio, Enjoying My Dream?

This decision tried my emotions, as I really loved Rio. Professionally, I was doing well, serving two years as the marketing and credit manager but wondered what'd be next in Brazil. VP Bob and Manager Armando enjoyed their positions, unlikely to move on. Chase Manhattan came calling but offered lateral positions and paid in cruzeiros, not dollars, as with Boston. I examined my pleasant life, which was perhaps less challenging than on arrival. Though my emotions said stay, my mind leaned toward accepting, if nothing more for career challenge and adventure. Yet, as hard as it'd be moving away from Rio, I wondered if my stay were but a phase?

Telling friends that I'd likely return to headquarters, I sensed their shock. They knew how much I loved their city, if not Boston. Graça was upbeat, wondering if she could join me abroad. I told Juvenal, who shed tears, saying, "You'll never return again." At my going-away party, Graça met another expatriate and travelled with him to Berlin. The last I'd heard, she began modeling in Lisbon but haven't had recent news. Juvenal stayed in Niteroi, across Guanabara Bay—married with two children, doing well this very day.

CHAPTER 5

Boston
(Parisian Interludes)

THANKSGIVING IN RIO was another tropical scorcher, bathers sweating on the beach. I arrived Boston in snow, people walking quickly, looking down from the wind. Shivering inside the cab, I sensed this move would be starker than imagined. UW friends let me a room in Cambridge, holding my hand in transition, not just in climate but in culture too.

On the Red Line, I commuted to the pregnant building downtown. At international, they hinted Uncle Frank would return to São Paulo in another head office move. Up a floor, I met Chad and multinational colleagues from London and Boston, adding my Latino touch to the crew.

They assigned me responsibility for Bacardi, Nashua, Schlumberger, Time Inc., Ely Lilly, Hewlett-Packard, Levi Strauss, Weyerhaeuser and PACCAR of Seattle. Multinational marketed bank services worldwide, using local currency loans as bait abroad to secure a relationship at home. Our goal was to become a part of the firm's domestic credit agreement, gaining kudos from bank higher-ups.

First calls were to company headquarters, meeting assistant treasurers of international and domestic finance. I'd ascertain firm treasury requirements, later calling on subsidiaries to satisfy specific needs. SchIumberger was the most sophisticated in tax and treasury planning, locating subs in havens to minimize liabilities. Its international treasury operations were in Paris and domestically in New York, with joint ventures around the world. Ideally, I'd visit as many as possible to secure closer relationships.

Bacardi was the most fun, with its international headquarters in Bermuda, holdings in the Bahamas, an importer in Miami, and a distillery in San Juan. I tried travelling away from New England's winter, as best I could. Yet returning to Boston found me bundling up and running for the T. At St. Paul's in Cambridge, I looked for the anonymous priest who listened that winter night but found a new pastor instead.

UW friends Jorge and Jan helped soothe my cultural withdrawal during Boston's long winter. They listened with empathy as I rambled on. Yet when Brazil's Milton Nascimento melodies plied the turntable, I'd excuse myself abruptly as tears streamed down. Outside winds howled, inside my heart was breaking, and Rio friends reappeared in dreams.

Spring arrived in fits and starts. Pedestrians swung their arms, looking up again. The north wind diminished its grip, and I sighed in relief. Warmer sunshine graced the city and budding leaves gave me hope. Walking down Charles Street on Beacon Hill, I noticed a For Sale sign inside a brownstone at Pickney and took a peek inside. I loved the condo on the first floor, attracted to its bay window, and closed on the spot. I'd often sit in this window to think, as well as to observe pedestrians passing by.

Summer was immensely enjoyable, so close to the Esplanade. I had a house warming on Independence Day, adjourning to Boston Pops along the Charles—so pleasant this time around. Along the river, I took up sailing and received visitors from Brazil. Life was slowly improving in Boston after the long winter. Yet summer fleeted by, transforming leaves to autumn colors. The breeze turned cooler from the north. Time to travel again, I mused, on my maiden trip to the City of Lights.

Schlumberger provided entrée to the Old Continent. I made visitations to client subsidiaries in London, Brussels, and Frankfurt, but I finally arrived in *la France*. My first glimpse of the Eiffel Tower proved emotional, as I recalled Edith Piaf and her tunes of lament. The bank reserved a hotel off Champs Elysees where its office was located. I met with BKB loan officers, including Bernard, who booked meetings and lunches at le Fouquet.

One evening, I crossed the bridge at St. Michel, and looked down on the Seine. A police boat was pulling someone from the river, so I asked a lady what happened in modest French.

She looked at me deeply, with sorrowful brown eyes, saying, "A young man jumped from the bridge, trying to commit suicide. They're trying to resuscitate him."

We saw the boat speed away and expressed hope they'd save his life. Then to this total stranger, I somehow confessed: "I once considered that fate myself. I felt there was no escape. My parents wanted me to stay in school, but it was tearing me apart. Had an anonymous priest not heard me out that winter night, I'm unsure I'd be here with you."

She listened carefully, her eyes glistening as we walked away, toward narrow streets of Saint Germain-des-Pres. "You were fortunate," she intoned, "but who listened to this young man?

"Are you new to Paris—could we speak further over a light repast?" she invited.

I followed her through the Latin Quarter to a Vietnamese bistro and spent a lovely evening with Eliane, despite this tragic moment.

The next day, Schlumberger's treasurer and assistant treasurer received me at their head office on St. Dominique. We chatted and adjourned to lunch. As devotees of French cuisine may attest, dining in Paris is beyond eating food. It is, rather, a delightful ordeal. We conversed without rush, taking time for an aperitif, hors d'oeuvres, delightful entrée, fruit and cheese, dessert and espresso—how civilized! Over dessert, we concluded an accord for more banking worldwide *entre nous*. Michel, the treasurer, connected me to managers around the world, boosting my exposure to this world-class oil service firm.

I bid adieu to Sclumberger, Eliane, and bank personnel, leaving Paris on a cloud. I continued my interludes in the City of Lights, along promenades and private rooms, delighting in its *joie de vivre!*

Back in Boston, I hunkered down as another winter set in. My dad's friend Paul invited me to dinner, where I confessed difficulty meeting native Bostonians, as most friends were from out of town. A 30 year resident, he admitted to few Boston friends, saying, "They don't need you."

I thought that odd, but he continued, "Bostonians have been here for generations with their own family and friends. Newcomers are tolerated but not needed." This native from North Carolina advised, "Especially in the privacy of their homes."

"The Casey family is the exception," I countered. "They invited me home in Dorchester, providing safe haven from HBS. I am so grateful to this day."

"Thank God for exceptions," Paul concluded. He reminded that ethnicity was important in dealings, as the Brahmans, Irish, Italians, Portuguese, and even French Canadians had contained social circles. *It was so different from Rio, Seattle, or Hawaii,* I mused, wondering how best I'd deal with my new identity as Irish Catholic.

Later, I returned to South America, starting in Buenos Aires. Downtown, I dodged restless pedestrians on Calle Florida, reaching Banco de Boston near Casa Rosada. Argentine beef was succulent, its Malbec superb, and tango after midnight a lively change. In Santiago, we visited vineyards and dined on seafood, revisiting Alberto's family too. In São Paulo, its entrepreneurial verve and movements were energizing, but still, Rio was the best.

Cariocas welcomed me with gusto over cafezinhos and chopps. Many asked how I liked headquarters, but I demurred, saying Boston's mentality was different from Brazil's. Branch colleagues kept me busy, visiting multinational firms and securing business. Friends sponsored lunch at Albamar, feasting on seafood and news, while watching ferries cross Guanabara Bay. We anticipated festivities for street kids that year with an Easter egg hunt, our Salgueiro family and bank friends helping out. *Saudades* is Brazilians' word for *nostalgia*, which I felt deeply on leaving Rio.

Another spring came, and summer flew by, with disturbing news from the home front: my dad was battling cancer. Having smoked many years, Dad's body and spirit were devastated. I went home in the summer and again in early fall, witnessing dear Dad pass in his hospital room, with some words unsaid. Our early relationship wasn't especially close, but it had improved later in life. Dad's "old country" tradition likely hardened his exterior, but his actions showed us love. Dad's entrepreneurship and zeal for justice and for travel rubbed off on his eldest son: Dad, thank you very much.

Winter seemed heavier, my dad's loss weighing down—especially later at night. Shouldn't I have said or done more while he was still alive? Bank friends noticed I was feeling down, and my boss wrote a letter to help pick me up. I attended Mass more often, having left the habit in recent years. I returned to St. Paul's, praying for that anonymous priest—and for dear Dad, just in case.

My routine included walking from Beacon Hill across the Commons, then meeting with multinational colleagues, presenting credit proposals, and calling clients all over the world. My BKB hero was Connie, of Germanic descent, whose unconventional thinking and flamboyance lit up our staid bank. As such bright lights were unusual, I became restless, seeking something new. The bank had a legacy in media lending, thanks to legendary Serge, who kept Warner Brothers afloat during the Great Depression. I proposed an international media survey, and Chad agreed, as long as I kept boosting my loan volume.

Eliane and I continued our long-distance liaison. Feeling lonelier upon Dad's death, I invited her to Boston, hoping for more meaningful relations.

Unfortunately, it was not to be. After the second month, we were getting on each other's nerves, arguing about most trivial concerns, like squeezing toothpaste in the middle versus rolling it up by its end. After a particularly tense night, my friend Jorge graciously invited Eliane home for her remaining stay. After this futile attempt, I wondered why it was it so difficult for me to live with another human being.

Looking for other ways to fill my time, the dean of Harvard's Kennedy School invited me to propose a noncredit course. The bank economist and I agreed to teach a weekly seminar on multinational firms' foreign policies in contrast to those of the Department of State. The dean agreed, and twenty-five students signed up, giving us positive reviews.

In mid-November, my mom made her first visit to Boston. We walked along Paul Revere's freedom trail and the Charles River, my old friend. I hosted a soiree for her in my Beacon Hill condo, attended by Uncle Frank, the Caseys, and friends. Mom enjoyed hearing stories about her eldest as her sadness seemed to lift.

Chad kindly let me mix business with pleasure, so I travelled to Bermuda, where Bacardi and Nashua had international offices. Bacardi's president made daiquiris to my mom's delight, and we concluded new opportunities in Spain and Venezuela. Nashua's Chris also charmed my mom with Aussie hospitality, sailing his forty-foot boat in Hamilton's bay. A delightful time, which helped heal both mother and son.

The next year, another fortuitous meeting took place. I'd sought insurance from local brokerages to increase export financing. When bank country limits were reached, BKB stopped lending to that country, unless another party assumed its political risk. Sandy's firm provided such insurance, enabling BKB to lend to exporters selling to Venezuela. BKB assumed the firm's credit risk, and the broker assumed Venezuela's country risk of default or illiquidity. Both sides prospered.

Since we'd consummated millions in deals with Sandy's firm, he invited me to his family home in gratitude. Little did I know that he was married to VP George H. W. Bush's sister, Nancy, who said that I should meet her nephew Jeb. She recounted how he'd married his Mexican sweetheart, loving Latin America like me. She called to connect us next time in Miami.

✳ ✳ ✳

In November 1982, I visited clients in LA, scoring an appointment in Hollywood. On its boulevard, I observed star names written, as well as signs that read, "Do Not Disturb," on sets on Paramount's lot. I asked for Paramount's president, Pay TV and Cable, and was ushered into a large office, with film posters and plaques adorning pastel walls. I spent a half hour with Mel, a marine vet himself, talking about international finance and showbiz.

I tried to convince Mel of BKB's media savvy, but he countered instead, "Steve, how long have you worked for the bank?"

"It'll be eleven years next year," I replied, intrigued.

"Then you're not a crook! They'd have found out by now," he said, continuing, "We need a dynamo like you in Latin America to set up video operations. Are you game?"

It didn't take me long to say sure, wondering what'd come next!

"Let me talk this over with my Universal counterpart, as we joint venture overseas. I'll get back to you." I thanked him, looked around this Hollywood studio, first viewed years ago.

I'd planned spending Thanksgiving with the Caseys but received a call Wednesday from Mel's assistant, saying, "You made a great impression, Steve. Mel would like to invite you to visit this Friday. Our worldwide video president is in town—can you come?"

I agreed and picked up tickets she'd wire—first class, of course! I drove to the Caseys for another wonderful Thanksgiving among their growing family after hosting their daughter, Julianne, at the bank. I returned to Boston for an overnight flight to LAX.

Checking into Universal City's Sheraton, I waited restlessly and called Mel's assistant. She noted my room and said, "Get some sunshine at the pool!" She called later, reconfirming dinner downstairs with Mel, Gene from Universal, and Roy from CIC Video at 6:00 p.m.

At the appointed hour, I waited outside, hearing Mel telling jokes. He introduced me to Gene, of darker Sicilian looks, and to the British Roy, who'd just arrived from Fiji. We talked a little, and they asked where I'd recommend setting up in Latin America. I replied, "How about Rio?"

Roy replied, "That sounds like fun!"

With that settled, they shared pleasantries and showbiz gossip over dinner. I was hardly in the conversation. I looked at my watch, showing 7:40 p.m., and asked if they had other questions, as my red-eye left at 9:00 p.m. They said, "No, but thank you for coming!"

On the flight back, I felt glum about the "interview," not one to tell many jokes. At least I flew first class. I returned to BKB subdued, my hopes asunder. A week passed without word, so I telephoned for any news.

"You made a great impression again, Steve. They'll send you a contract—congratulations!" she exclaimed. I was flabbergasted but happy, awaiting their draft. In Hollywood, no one worked without a contract, from the lowest assistant to the VP of Latin America. It was important to heed all details, so a friendly attorney offered counsel. He suggested an annual contract, renewable, with starting salary at $85K, a third more than BKB. Mel called to say they'd agreed to my salary, and would send a contract from Amsterdam.

In the meantime, I received a call from Michel of Schlumberger, saying he'd visit New York the following week: Would I join him for dinner? I agreed and met him, his assistant treasurer, and the CFO of their worldwide joint venture at Manny's Steak House.

They applauded my efforts at the bank and invited BKB into their US revolving credit agreement—a real coup! Over dessert, Michel advised the assistant treasurer post of their worldwide operations in Paris was vacant—would I be interested? *Wow*, I thought, *when it rains, it pours*—two offers within a week! I said that I'd consider their thoughtful proposal but disclosed that I'd received another offer as well.

Turning Point: Go to the City of Lights as Assistant Treasury or Return to the Marvelous City at a Start-Up?

How could I choose among two dream offers demanding immediate response? On return to Boston, only Jorge knew my quandary, having housed Eliane the previous year. Were our relationship more in sync, I'd likely accepted Schlumberger's tempting offer in the City of Lights. Yet Rio's spirit was in my blood and in my dreams, having taken me out of my American box.

So I stewed through mid-December, tempted again to return to the edge. But was a new experience in Paris more daring than starting from scratch video businesses south of the border? I pondered how blasé I'd become in banking and wondered if negotiating on the other side of the table would be that novel. I'd always yearned to enter showbiz, so might not this be my moment?

Unlike previous crossroads, I sensed no sign from beyond, so I pondered what my father would do. After all, he'd started up his own business, fighting for his niche among the big boys, with apparent success. How would I best follow suit?

The following day, I called Michel in Paris and declined his offer, affirming that I'd change careers from finance to show business. He wished me well, asking where I'd be going and how Boston's relationship would fare. I promised him proper transition and told him I'd always be available to discuss *l'Amérique latine*. The bank was happy that I'd secured BKB into Schlumberger's domestic line, though unhappy I'd take more time away.

By late January, the contract hadn't arrived from CIC's general counsel in Amsterdam, but a first-class ticket had. I was invited to attend Paramount and Universal's board meeting of CIC Video, its worldwide joint venture.

Due to US antitrust concerns, they held such meetings offshore, to avoid engaging in collusive behavior stateside. In 1983, the board meeting was held in Netherlands, where the VP-elect of Latin America was asked to present—still without contract.

As Chad had moved up BKB's ladder, Skip was multinational's new boss and heard rumblings of my looking outside. I asked him for five days leave and said that on return, I should have some news, thanking him for understanding.

I flew into Amsterdam International, admiring the city's well-developed canals. A Paramount chauffeur was waiting outside to take me to a chic hotel along its main canal. Paramount and Universal upper management attended the board meeting, enjoying camaraderie while discussing strategy and marketing—especially in home video, the latest source of Hollywood revenue. Later, battles ensued between theatrical and video partisans.

CIC Video wanted videocassettes sold simultaneous to film's theatrical exhibition, while cinema partisans argued for longer windows to protect their revenues. As home video and cable TV gained popularity among viewers, theatrical people felt under siege. This cause célèbre forced spirited debates—name-calling included—over windows for hot movies, such as *Flashdance* or *Scarface*.

Eventually, both sides tired of this war of words. The twenty execs turned toward me for respite and to size up their new hire. I gave my brief bio, describing my time in Brazil and Boston, as well as how I shared Dad's entrepreneurial DNA.

"My dad battled the big boys in business and succeeded. For Paramount and Universal, we'll need to persevere against piracy, bureaucracy, and inflation—constant foes in Latin America."

"Are you up to the job?" inquired Paramount's theatrical head.

"After Vietnam and Brazil, I'll go forward with confidence. My parents also taught me not to bow to other mortals. Only to God."

"Where do you think we should start up?" inquired Universal's exec.

"Brazil and Mexico are the two home-run markets, where I will dedicate time. Other markets, while important, are but singles and doubles," I affirmed.

"How do you plan to proceed? You've not been in show business before," persisted Paramount's lawyer.

"Over decades, I've developed personal relationships south of the border. I have a can-do spirit and can push to the edge. I will not fail you."

I sat down to applause, Mel congratulating for thinking fast on my feet. Overlooking the canal in the candlelit bar, he, Gene, and Roy raised their glasses and signed the contract before me. They said their counsel would send me a copy. They said video windows could be from two to six months, but cautioned that I'd have to politick with theatrical counterparts to make it happen.

On return to Boston, multinational colleagues asked what was going on. Come March, I'd received a personal invite to attend a Stanford International–Hudson Institute conference on "The Future of Brazil." Relations at the bank had become tense, as I awaited copy of the contract from Amsterdam. I told my boss that I'd been invited to this conference because of my Brazilian connections but would raise the BKB flag for a couple of days. I said that I'd take leave, if he thought best, and excused my absence again. He reluctantly agreed but wanted definition ASAP.

At the Brazil conference along the Hudson, I met the Institute's founder, who seemed half asleep, only to awaken with perceptive questions, keeping speakers on their toes. I mentioned that Brazil was entering a hangover phase, taking on debt to fuel past miracles. Its people were hardworking, resilient, and entrepreneurial, I affirmed. Its economy grew at night, since many Brazilians had other sidelines to their day job.

Several attended from other think tanks, universities, and the Department of State. I was the only banker invited and enjoyed rubbing elbows with cognoscenti of this slumbering giant.

On The Edge

Back at BKB, some wondered if I'd gone overboard. I asked myself if my desire to enter showbiz might have stretched me beyond prudence. I kept my head down, waiting. On my birthday, the signed contract finally arrived. So I took that leap of faith into another career.

Victory for student body office is cheered by brothers at Phi Kappa Psi, University of Washington, spring 1964. *Courtesy of WA Alpha.*

Family celebrates UW graduation and acceptance to Harvard Business School, summer 1966.
Photographic section assembled by RickEdelmanPhotography. Photos without annotation are from author's personal collection.

The Casey family provided refuge from HBS, Boston, 1967.

Baker Library, Harvard Business School. *Courtesy: Larry K. Fish.*

Fr. Fulton gives blessing before heading to Vietnam, spring 1968. *Courtesy: Blessed Sacrament.*

Ensign Murphy in gun director, near the Demilitarized
Zone, Vietnam, 1969.

USS Goldsborough (DDG 20) on mission offshore Vietnam, 1968.
Photo by PH2 Wyckoff, U.S. Navy.

Alma Mater sculpture of the goddess Athena, stands before Low Library,
Columbia University. *Photo by author.*

Brothers Edwin and Richar serve as guides to Columbia University students,
Plaza de Armas, Cuzco, Peru, 1971. *Photo by Allan Little.*

Ethereal Rio de Janeiro, Brazil, from Sugar Loaf. *Courtesy: Marco Marquez.*

Cousin Pat and author shake the 'Red Room' spread, Copacabana, Rio de Janeiro, 1978.

Salgueiro brothers and family play samba, on the path up the hill. Tijuca, Rio de Janeiro, 1974.

Salgueiro family, left to right: Almir, father Moacyr, Steve, mother Severina, brothers Ino and Buddha, Rio de Janeiro, 1974.
Courtesy: de Andrade family.

Steve and Graça stood out in soirees and on social pages, Rio de Janeiro, 1977.

Courtesy: Reinaldo's studios, Rio de Janeiro, 1977.

Juvenal teaching capoeira.

Resting on the *sobrado*'s window, Copacabana.

Steve on flute, Juvenal on berimbau. Rio de Janeiro, 1978.

Uncle Frank and his lovely wife, Dora, Boston, 1983.

Original headquarters, the First National Bank of
Boston, Boston. *Courtesy: William F. Hamilton.*

Dad shows off his beloved Cessna, Paine Field.

Paramount Pictures display at the
American Film Market, Los Angeles, 1987.

CIC Video licensees at the first Latin American Conference, Bariloche,
Argentina, 1986. Marcos is third from left, Steve in the middle.

Cynthia Rhodes inaugurates Paramount and Universal's joint venture with *Flashdance* home video, Caracas, Venezuela, 1983. She starred in *Staying Alive* the same year. *Courtesy: Blan-CIC Video.*

Giving out Christmas presents, the hill of Salgueiro, Tijuca, Rio de Janeiro, 1984.

A TV public service announcement created a huge demand for the kid's party, *Casa de Estive*, Rio de Janeiro, 1984.

Sheldon and Steve out on the town, Washington DC, 1989.

Jack Valenti, founder and longtime president, Motion Picture Association of America, "made the call, and made the difference" inside the Beltway. Washington DC, 1989. *Courtesy: Motion Picture Association.*

Honorable Elizabeth Dole led delegation to El Salvador, Washington DC, 2002. *Courtesy: Ambassador Leon.*

To Steve Murphy
With best wishes, *Geo Bush* *Barbara Bush*

To Steve Murphy —
Thank you for your advice, counsel, support and friendship.
June 1992   Sincerely, Andy Card

Courtesy: the White House, President George H. W. Bush, Washington DC,
1992.

Jeb Bush for **Governor**

11-12-94.

Dear Steve,

Thank you so much for your letter! The defeat was hard ... we should have known. life goes on. Again, thanks your help. Sincerely, Jeb

Jeb! PD. FOR JEB BUSH FOR GOVERNOR 1994

Jeb Bush —— for —— Governor

Courtesy: the Jeb Bush for Governor campaign. Miami, 1994.

Professor Terry with brother, Muscat, Oman, 1997.

Sister Pamela, mom and Steve at family home, Seattle, 1989.

Kids kick ball to the gringo goalie - goal? Tecate, Mexico, 2000.

Seattle U students and professors on study mission, Rio de Janeiro, 1998.

Mass under the mango tree, Fr. Owen officiated. Namitembo, Malawi, 2001.

Peace Corps volunteer Michael Wunsch, worked miracles with his community raising 'bok choy', el Cantoral, Honduras, 2002.

I proposed and Vicki said yes! Snoqualmie Falls Lodge, February 2002.

Vicki and Steve at Tidal Basin, Washington DC, 2002.

Our honeymoon luncheon at La Bastille bistro,
with Eliane (left) and chef (right), Paris, February 2003.

Fidel peering over shoulders of Steve, Vice Dean Fidel and Professor
Jose Antonio, University of Havana, 2015.

Brothers proudly show off their private Packard taxi, financed by
Miami cousins.

The Cathedral of the Virgin Mary of the Immaculate Conception, *Habana Vieja*.

Sprucing up the façade of a new *paladar* bistro in Old Havana.

Alfonso's 'coco-cab'. We pushed it up steeper inclines along *el Malecón,* Havana, Cuba.

This trio played for tourists in Havana but looked for gigs in Miami. *La Moneda Cubana,* Havana, 2015.

CHAPTER 6
Return to Rio

THE FLIGHT TO Brazil was choppy and clouds shrouded Corcovado, over-looking Rio de Janeiro. Seeing this illuminated statue of Cristo had always given me a sense of hope. As the plane landed at Galeão, cloaked in gray, I wondered what lay ahead in this city I loved: Would it be the same?

To avoid haggling with the cabbie, I purchased a voucher inside the airport. The cab sped through two tunnels under Corcovado, separating Rio's poorer northern neighborhoods from glamorous beaches in the South Zone. Around the Lagoa, we raced, entering Copacabana's backside and climbed up slippery cobblestones to my apartment on the hill.

Earlier, I'd written my renter, advising my intended return. He looked unhappy that Sunday morning, ushering me to the red room. After perfunctory words, he left to the bedroom and I down the street, hoping to view the famous beach. Rain was still falling, and Copacabana looked empty, save vendors shivering under tarps. Rain affected cariocas, dampening mood and spirit, keeping them inside small apartments and not on the openness of the beach. That morning I didn't dive into Rio's waters, as was my habit. Instead, I ran for a beachfront café, seeking warmth and conversation from blasé waiters.

The next day, I took a cool bus downtown to meet the theatrical manager of Paramount, Universal, and MGM/UA's joint venture, called United International Pictures. Its offices overlooked Cinelandia's mosaic sidewalks and cinemas, with moviegoers and petty thieves sharing space. I went up to UIP's Brazilian headquarters on floor 23 and met an assistant, who said the manager was busy.

I returned later and met a short man in his late sixties, with a scowl on his face, looking skeptically over rim glasses at this unknown thirty-nine-year-old. I tried at small talk but received short word answers in return. I switched to diplomacy and asked, "Can't theatrical and video business thrive side by side, Sr. Paulo, benefiting each other and the studios we represent?"

"Movies should be seen on the large screen. I don't like video, and neither do my people. Theaters and video are rivals. We are not friends," he said, his jowls shaking in anger.

The interview over, I left downcast, unwelcome in my new showbiz gig. His assistant smiled sympathetically, saying his bark was worse than his bite. She led me downstairs to my authorized office, in a squat building behind theatrical's high-rise. In the back alley, we entered this warehouse of film reels, signage, and cinema posters. On its darkened second floor was an empty room, offered to house the VP of Latin America to initiate Paramount and Universal video activities.

In Brazil, news wasn't much brighter. Its first civilian elected president in decades had died from hospital infection instead of assuming office. An unknown VP stepped into place. Inflation ramped up again, doubling to a 60 percent annual rate. Merchants felt uncertain about Brazil's future and raised prices, squeezing families on the edge. I checked with my family on the hill. They were happy about my return but sad that son Almir had lost his job and that their samba school hadn't won Carnaval. It was a different Rio this time around, not the idyllic homecoming I longed to receive.

With frosty receptions at both home and work, I cloistered myself in the upstairs office, recalling my closet at Columbia Business School. I hired an assistant, Luciana, who provided excellent company and dealt ably with older, theatrical employees at UIP. She offered a female touch to our rustic space, with flowers and posters, more welcoming to infrequent visitors. She found a nice desk and chair that leaned back, even permitting me to stretch out. Slowly, relations with UIP staffers improved, but not UIP's GM for Brazil, still at war with video encroaching his turf.

To break out of this malaise, I called on shakers and movers in Rio's showbiz, starting with the Motion Picture Association of America. My namesake and former BKB colleague was executive assistant to the MPAA's VP of Latin America. Steve welcomed me home and looked forward to having two Hollywood allies to do battle with video pirates, occupying most commercial space.

He introduced me to his boss, Harry, a resident for years and renowned in Rio's social circles. Harry invited me to *Flashdance*'s screening, saying Rio's beautiful people would be present. He seemed pleased to have another *americano* to raise Hollywood's profile in Brazil's stagnant theatrical market. Because of many years in Rio, some Brazilians gossiped that Harry was the CIA's agent in place. They still attended his cocktail parties and screenings with gusto, enjoying Harry's *savoir faire*.

I also met with Brazilian movie directors, Luiz Carlos and Lucy, to create a common front against the pirates—especially in the media. They invited me to soirees in their penthouse near Rio's governor's mansion, pitching movie deals over *caipirinhas*. Sometimes I'd cross Harry in these affairs, and he'd asked about my social life: "How do you find your return to Rio, this time around?"

"It feels edgier, Harry. I sense more danger on Rio's streets," I replied.

"And with Paulo, are you getting by? He's sometimes prickly."

"I don't think he likes me. He told me how he hates video," I confided.

"Forget Brazil for the moment, Steve. Go to Caracas instead. Tony and Lenora are more open-minded to new media," he counseled.

My boss in London approved my trip to Venezuela, where I'd once visited Sclumberger's sub. Flying business class to Caracas, I arrived early morning at La Guaira airport and noticed hillside communities like Rio's favelas. An angry driver in a big Ford Galaxy shouted at pedestrians crossing the highway toward the Caracas Hilton, which was overbooked. They rerouted me to its homey Anauco residence, where both Venezuelan families and hotel visitors lived.

A big Chevrolet drove me to UIP's offices in La Sabana Grande, honking at other American gas-guzzlers. Big cars symbolized Venezuela's wealth as an oil exporter, and the locals filled their tanks at less than a dollar per gallon. I also learned a new Spanish word, *chevere*, borrowing from the English word *Chevrolet*, meaning something "cool" in local parlance.

At their offices, full of posters, Tony and Lenora welcomed me as a brother-in-arms, hugging in the traditional greeting south of the border. After an extended meet and greet with staff over *cafecito*, they took me to their favorite *trattoria* and recounted their story. They'd arrived in Venezuela as Cuban refugees after Castro came to power, working their way up in show business. With sweat equity, they'd bought theaters with local partners and became known as reliable exhibitors in an unreliable market.

As they showed Paramount, Universal, and MGM/UA films in their theaters, London tapped them as UIP's joint venture partner in film distribution. This relationship gained show time for studios in dicey Venezuela and prestige for this power couple in international markets like Cannes and LA. They became the go to impresarios in South American show business.

Over lunch, we talked about families, UIP politics, personalities, and tricks of the trade. Over dessert and espresso, we got to business, agreeing to another joint venture in video, similar to UIP. Over cognac, we decided to call the firm "Blan-CIC Video," after their surname and CIC, Paramount and Universal's video venture name in London.

We toasted again and discussed windows from theatrical release to video sales, agreeing on two months for blockbusters and a month for less popular films. Another advantage of Tony and Lenora as partners was their control of film distribution and exhibition and now video, compressing windows and avoiding theatrical fights like in Brazil.

I telexed our proposal to CIC's head office, receiving approval the next day. We spent time visiting TV stations in Caracas, eager to promote legal home video as long as they got a cut from direct sales. We visited pirate video stores to peruse Hollywood films on display. We talked about legal strategy to combat video thieves, which didn't remove CIC films from their shelves. Attorneys from the MPAA, Paramount, and Universal began prosecuting pirates. Blan-CIC's role was to provide commercial alternatives to consumers and stores.

Flying back to Rio, I marveled how differently Tony and Lenora embraced new media to complement theatrical release. I returned to my lowly office, feeling upbeat, and I shared the good news with our small staff. Telexing all UIP managers in Latin America, I highlighted our new venture with this power couple, encouraging them to sound out exhibitors, distributors, and TV stations. CIC Video was ready to wheel and deal.

Over cocktails, Harry congratulated me: "Well done, Steve. I understand Tony and Lenora treated you well."

"Superb, Harry. Thanks for the lead. Where should I set my sights next? I still feel stymied in Brazil," I replied.

""Be patient, Steve. Brazil will come around. There's always Mexico to think about."

Socially, my life had been minimal, as I just liberated myself from renters. Graça was still in Europe with a German producer, and Juvenal was across the bay with his high school girlfriend. At the Ford Foundation, I met *simpatico* Michael, who enjoyed hosting *feijoadas* on Saturdays late into evening. Zezé often attended in company with Afro-Brazilian friends who were struggling to make it in Brazilian show business.

Without permanent liaison, I started hitting the streets—not always with favorable results. In seeking new experiences, I accepted an invite to witness *macumba* in Rio's suburbs in the North Zone. Macumba was Rio's version of black magic, calling spirits from the underworld to redress issues of the living. Often, an aggrieved party asked a medium to cast spells on an aggressor or a disloyal lover, participating in a séance of percussion, incense, and chants to beckon spirits to come down.

We arrived in the hot bus to the North Zone, sweating profusely, and entered a brick building under a tin roof. Congo drums were already stirring emotions and spirits, with seven "aunts" dressed in white, smoking cigars, and twirling in rhythm. Thirty people circled around, clapping to drum beats and emitting strange sounds.

The medium was a slight, dark man with indigenous traces, dressed in white with red beads around his neck. He twisted and turned, his body shaking violently as he "received the saint." The spirit possessed his body, making it tremble and caw like a crow, assuming unusual shapes. Otherworldly sounds and foam emanated from his mouth. One aunt in white swooned to the floor, rescued by handlers, then another, while the drums pounded on. I felt unsettled and afraid—it didn't feel right.

Outside, I was hyperventilating, and my friend asked if I was all right. I replied that I was unsure but had to go home. He offered to join me, but I said I'd unwind alone, taking two hot busses back to the South Zone. I staggered up my cobblestone street, without greeting neighbors, seeking refuge in my *sobrado*. I opened all the windows in hopes that macumba spirits would leave, still sensing a presence weighing down.

This backsliding Catholic then dropped to his knees, desperately calling on the Holy Spirit to rescue me—such was my fear. I breathed deeply and rhythmically, and I finally fell into slumber late afternoon. I dreamt of crows and vipers battling in surrealistic form and awoke at midnight in a sweat—hoping to be alone.

Fortunately, Sunday morning arrived, and skies cleared. I jogged down, past the Catholic parish to Copacabana's beach, diving under breaking waves. For me, ocean waters cleansed me, as worldly woes seemed to wash away. That day, I was thankful for the Atlantic and prayed that those macumba spirits go away. I vowed to never again seek that way. For this moment of trouble, I took God out of the box, hoping I'd survive another day.

I awoke on Monday, feeling better yet not 100 percent. At work, Luciana asked if I was feeling OK. I said I needed a second cup of coffee, not wanting to recall my horrible weekend. Fortunately, I immersed myself in telex responses from my group mail. UIP managers in Mexico and Colombia agreed to present me to local groups—would I like to visit?

My boss telexed that he'd fly down to Blan-CIC Video's inauguration in Caracas, confirming MPAA actions against pirates there. Both TV networks showed raids on illegal duplication facilities in Caracas and Maracaibo, with glum pirates in police vans. The *Hollywood Reporter* reported these actions, a precursor to Paramount and Universal's video entry in Venezuela. We'd be the first major studios in South America's video market.

Thanks to our Venezuelan power couple, Cynthia Rhodes of *Flashdance* and *Staying Alive* visited from Hollywood, delighting us with her grace and charm. Even video-store owners attended our fiesta, smiling at Cynthia and promising legal Paramount and Universal videos on their shelves.

My boss offered kudos and encouraged me toward other markets, while Brazil stood still. After winding down the festivities, I agreed to fly to Bogota at 8,300 feet.

Towering peaks overshadowed Colombia's capital, nestled in a valley. The CIC manager brought me to the Tequendama, where business deals occurred, despite edginess at night. Bombs had gone off nearby, as guerillas acted against government troops and buildings. Despite such danger, Bogota's residents got on with daily life. Their Spanish was a pleasure to hear, and their people produced beauties of Andean mystique. At night, they danced cumbia and welcomed this gringo to join in.

We visited RCN, Caracol TV stations, and an exhibitor, Cine Colombia. We enjoyed pleasant lunches at country clubs and promises for proposals. I thought politic to license our catalogue to a Colombian group, as CIC's manager didn't have Tony and Lenora's clout. Despite fewer VCRs than Venezuela, Colombia had future potential from its larger population. Hollywood executives didn't visit for safety concerns, so I encouraged Ivan of Cine Colombia to submit an offer ASAP. I left Bogota feeling upbeat and flew overnight to Rio again.

Our staff was ecstatic with CIC's opening but wondered when Brazil would start up. In addition to UIP's opposition, Brazilian authorities created hurdles, requiring legal distributors to release 25 percent in Brazilian films. Yet video stores could stock pirate films as they saw fit. There were few Brazilian hits like *Dona Flor and Her Two Husbands*, most garnering little audience. The exceptions were *pornochanchadas*, offering T & A and racy sex. London balked and encouraged me elsewhere—this time, Mexico's way.

Mexico City at Christmas is one of the most festive places on earth, its *posadas* and poinsettias gracing neighborhoods. In the hemisphere's largest city, I attended one posada, where a couple dressed as Mary and Joseph walked the street, calling for lodging for baby Jesus. Such ceremonies could continue until Christmas Eve, but on this night, a homeowner opened her doors and bade them enter. Colorful piñatas, filled with sweets representing human downfalls, were strung above. Blindfolded kids would hit them amid cheers, pouring out treats from broken sides. "*Feliz Navidad!*" they cheered.

In between posadas, I visited TV networks, film distributors, and producers to sound out interest. Luncheons began around 3:00 p.m. and ended after sundown, with courses of exquisite cuisine, so different from Tex-Mex. After such a lunch at a distributor's country club, we returned to his smart offices in Polanco. The owner went inside, while I waited in the reception with a sad office boy.

I asked, "Amigo, *que pasa?*"

Quietly he replied, "They haven't paid me in three weeks, *americano*, and Christmas is near. What am I to do?"

"*Feliz Navidad*," I offered, with some *pesos*, wondering about this firm, which had so wined and dined me. I later discovered that this distributor had loans overdue and a reputation to impress out-of-town gringos to secure film catalogues for a song. Thus, I learned another lesson—to speak with employees at all levels of company hierarchy, including this office boy who offered his heads up.

Fernando of Televisa picked me up after New Year's Eve in his own BMW, with two bodyguards in back. I noticed a bulge at his ankle, which housed a snub-nosed .38 pistol.

"You can't be too careful, Mr. Paramount," he said.

We arrived to his offices at Mexico's number-one TV network, with armed guards at doors and hallways to rebuff kidnapping attempts on wealthy execs. We had a power breakfast in its executive dining room, with officers and family members present. Fernando did most of the talking: "We want to break the pirates' backs in Mexico. We have close relations with the police and government. We'll televise all the busts on nationwide TV. Pirates will think twice about crossing us. Socially and practically, it will not serve them well."

On Epiphany Sunday, or Day of Kings, as celebrated around Latin America, I went to Mass with the family of my Columbia classmate, José Antonio, near Coyoacán. He reminded me how influential this TV family was in Mexico—even the government relied on them. "They'd be a powerful ally," he said.

The next day, I reported back to London, which gave me the green light to negotiate a licensing deal, which I did with Televisa, fixing $10,000 a film in minimum guarantee (MG) and a 35 percent royalty on each video sold. Studios usually required licensees to pay an MG per film before sending its master, from which video copies were made. As sales against this film title occurred, royalties were discounted against the MG. If royalties surpassed the minimum, studios received overages, controlled tightly by royalty reports and studio accountants. This licensing MO is still commonplace in Hollywood.

Returning to Rio on wonderful Varig airline, I was flying high. Our CIC team garnered positive PR with another big deal but asked when Brazil would come on line. Harry gave me kudos at an MPAA screening, knowing all the details, of course.

My MPAA namesake planned a new coalition, the Union of Brazilian Video (UBV), including film producers, distributors, and video companies like ours, to battle pirates and regulatory authorities alike. Inflation ramped up and families suffered throughout Brazil. Inflation psychology took hold of businesses, which stocked scarce goods, like videotapes, raising prices every week.

Rio's summer returned to sweltering days and tropical languor. After work, I'd pass by Casa Simpatia, wondering where Beto had gone. In Copacabana, I'd stop by Quixote in Posto 2, for chopps and a sandwich. Later, I'd walked along Avenida Atlantica, seeking ocean breezes and inviting looks.

On weekends, I'd hit the beach and hang out with the volleyball crowd, getting burned if I didn't watch out. They'd call me "lobster" or "tomato" at my red, gringo look—my Northern Hemisphere genes withering under scorching sun. Personal rendezvous were brief and inconsistent. So I dove deep into work, hiding an emptiness within. Professionally, though, things still seemed good.

Instead of Carnaval, I headed south to Buenos Aires to meet another film distributor who owned cinemas as well. Rabeno had heard about Tony and Lenora's accord and wanted in. After days of haggling over Argentinean beef and Malbec wine, we reached a deal: $5,000 in MG and 38 percent in royalty. This group presciently hired a former pirate as its video manager and ably attacked the market, with MPAA legal actions helping out. I lingered more days, savoring Mendoza's wines and Bariloche's beauty, where we hosted an all Latin America conference the following year.

Back at home base, our little staff was feeling prime, having launched three video enterprises last year with more on the horizon. Our *enfant terrible*, Brazil, still held us back. Its galloping inflation, bureaucracy, and piracy weighed us down. The newly created UBV group pleaded with distributors to enter the market where pirates reaped high returns. Only Globo Video released movies—mostly independent US, European, and Brazilian films. Paulo seemed grumpier than usual as video took off around the world, though not in his backyard. Harry was his ebullient self, rising above the fray and appearing in society pages as the year rolled on.

Before Christmas, I met with Roberto, the eldest son of the family that owned TV Globo, the world's third largest TV network. He offered help for another party for Rio's street kids and aired public service announcements, requesting donations of food, clothing, and toys at the *casa de Estive* in Copacabana.

Instead, hundreds of Rio's kids scampered up our cobblestone street, scaring neighbors used to smaller events. Sponsors like McDonalds, Coca-Cola, Habib, BankBoston, Bicicletas Caloi, and Julio provided another "miracle of the loaves," so every kid got a present, Big Mac, Coke, and hug from Papai Noel. Christmas Day, TV Globo followed me up Salgueiro's hill, where we shared remaining gifts.

Interviewing for its evening newscast, *Jornal Nacional*'s reporter asked, "Why do you, an *americano*, hand out gifts to Brazilian children?"

On nationwide TV, I replied, "I love the Brazilian people. It's the least I can do for our street kids."

My Salgueiro brother added, "It's Christmas—they want to be happy too."

New Year's Eve arrived as thousands of cariocas, dressed in white, entered Atlantic waters along Copacabana's beach. Several launched floats to the goddess of the sea, Iemanjá, celebrated as a reawakening in Rio, January 1. In Bahia, they'd wait until February 2 to honor Yoruba's "mother whose children are *pisces*" and "mother of all spirits" in the nations of Candomblé. Brazil took spirits seriously.

Midnight, I entered those waters and observed spectacular fireworks cascading down Hotel Meridien, while carousing with revelers until dawn broke on Atlantic waters.

Another year began, and London grew impatient about Latin America's largest market. Roy and Brian flew down, along with Universal's Charley and MPAA bigwigs to plot strategy. We visited Globo Video's manager, who offered to license our entire catalogue, using TV ads to sell videocassettes. Roy was skeptical, sensing they'd want to corner the market, hindering growth of this new media. Interviewing other potential partners, we found them without finances or moxie to start up.

"Maybe it's time to go it alone," I asserted.

"Steve, do you really think you can? Brazil's a complicated place," my boss demurred.

"Why not?" I said. Then I added, "We'll need your help in London to deal with Paulo, who's still pushing back."

In São Paulo, we visited its most sophisticated pirate, who vowed to leave "wayward ways" if he could duplicate our films, including CIC inspectors inside his facility.

"We'll consider your offer, Tony, but actions speak louder than words," I said. To show good faith, that duplicator had a literal "fire sale" of pirated Paramount and Universal videos. In return, he became our strategic ally, slowly turning the market toward legal films.

I recommended setting up in São Paulo but somehow picked up hepatitis from my own wayward ways. Quarantined in my Copa apartment, I conducted business by phone, answering telexes that CIC's assistant dropped by. At night, I'd hold video sessions for neighbors, CIC employees, or whoever showed up starting 8:00 p.m.

At home, I interviewed both Marcos and Marques to become marketing manager and controller for CIC's start up. Marcos, having worked for Globo Video, was well connected to the market. Marques was a savvy navigator of Brazil's complex maze of cascading taxes and government bureaucracy. The media later dubbed us "the Three Musketeers of video." We've kept our friendship until the present day, enjoying our annual *feijoada* at Rubaiyat.

Inaugurating *CIC Video* in the Garden District of São Paulo, Brazil's media acclaimed a "new age of entertainment." We sponsored *Flashdance* contests around Brazil, with the winners scoring auditions at Paramount's studios before Hollywood execs. A young man and woman won the prize and showed off their break dance moves, before disappearing into greater

LA's maze. Marcos moved aggressively with the video clubs: buy CIC's videos, or face the *policia militar.*

TV Globo publicized police raids, which did the trick, showing pirates looking sheepishly at cameras, while being handcuffed by cops. Video club owners, concerned about social appearances, didn't cotton to negative PR. CIC sales skyrocketed, encouraging other studios to take the plunge, like Warner Brothers. Studio execs and London were delighted, renewing my contract with a bonus to boot.

With Brazil underway, I travelled to smaller markets like Uruguay, Chile, Peru, and Ecuador, spending two-thirds of my time on the road. Nocturnal partners slipped inside my hotel rooms, while I negotiated by day with showbiz execs. Travelling in business or first class, I felt on top of the world, gaining kudos in Hollywood's media as well.

Only in Panama did things turn squirrely. Angry at our actions against piracy, Noriega's goons beat on GC Charley's door at the Hilton, while I listened nearby. Only when Universal's GC threatened to call the US embassy did they relent, though they pursued us in other ways. CIC eventually licensed an Argentinean in Colon's Free Trade Zone, relatively safe from caudillo thugs. Later when President Bush invaded Panama to depose Noriega, we discovered his racket's broad reach—trafficking drugs, humans, and pirated films around the hemisphere. A bad dude, whom we fortuitously avoided in brief forays.

As another year peeled away, I wondered what might be next, having established ten video operations in barely four years. Piracy, though present, was on the wane, as more studios entered markets. Briefly, Paramount friends spoke about my working in LA, but I didn't feel the urge, as Brazil's market blasted off. Marcos and I talked about initiating our own distribution company, as long as I'd guarantee his monthly stipend. He had a growing family and was concerned about steady income. I took pause at such responsibility and saw stock values crash later that year.

CIC's Argentinean lawyer, dubbed "Diego Maradona," ferreted our intentions, alerting CIC in London. Relations with Roy proved testy, so I said Marcos would do ably as Brazil's GM instead. Reluctantly, I moved on from CIC, hanging out on the limb.

I hastily conceived plan B to begin video distribution in São Paulo with the nephew of CIC's Uruguayan distributor. He backed out at the last moment, so I started Tropical Enterprises solo to buy film rights from independent US producers, relicensing them to Brazilian distributors. I also consulted for two large Brazilian groups, negotiating with US majors, but Brazilians balked at hard currency obligations, while inflation ratcheted to 30 percent a month.

My BKB amigo, James, let me stay in his apartment in São Paulo's red zone, as he'd begun business there, commuting to Rio on weekends. The stock market crash of 1987 then broke my finances with my mood following suit. I engaged in risky behavior, wondering where it'd all end.

As another year began, I wandered Rio's beach and wrote:

I see my tracks on wet sand...but only memories remain. I walk along Copacabana, looking back at fresh imprints, some erased by the sea, some confused by others' steps, some smoothed by the wind's caress. I wonder if my tracks are like my actions and words, leaving traces in the minds of others, but displaced by events more pressing. How hard I've tried, I now realize, to leave my little mark on humanity through this prose, past poems, future paintings. While I may persevere longer, the scythe of time will prove enduring, o'er those footprints in the sand.

That year I was blessed by visits from Seattle friends, especially my UW hero, Prof. Costigan and his wife, who stopped in Rio on a cruise. I walked with them from the port to Casa Simpatia, where a decade ago, Beto once played his samba on my shoes. I told his story, and the professor observed,

"I'm proud of you Stephen. At least you heard the shoeshine boy's lament. You did an act of kindness, and that's important."

I confessed to him about the anonymous priest's counsel to seek the small things in life that one lonely night.

"I'm not a religious man," he said, "but I'd like to converse with him. Maybe some clergy have evolved of late." He thanked me for my Christmas missives and UW tome written on graduation, "*Je Pense, Donc Je Suis.*" He said that they still bicycled in the university district but felt unsure about Rio's streets.

I concurred and bid them well. To this legendary professor, whom I'd met in Irish History class and at UW's debate featuring him versus William F. Buckley Jr., I take off my hat.

My life went on, back and forth to São Paulo, falling into casual encounters and occasional deals. I still kept God in a box, not wanting to disturb my lifestyle, despite its reduced state. My hope was waning until November arrived. Vice President Bush was just elected president of the United States.

Jeb had mentioned that if I wanted to serve the new Administration, "now was the time." Every administration had two thousand political appointments to offer the faithful—especially when one party took over from another. In this instance, President-elect Bush followed President Reagan of the GOP, with fewer political plums forthcoming. However, what did I have to lose? I bought a round-trip ticket to Washington, DC, to throw my little hat into the ring.

Unfortunately, the White House personnel's young transition team did not know me from Adam, losing the letter Jeb had written. I left dejected but met my friend Fritz at the MPAA, who introduced me to Jack Valenti, DC's most powerful lobbyist. Fritz told how I'd battled pirates and initiated Paramount and Universal's operations throughout Latin America. Jack replied, "I like your energy. This administration could use someone like you."

Feeling better, a DC friend recalled my meeting the new Deputy Chief of Staff in Boston—would he remember me? I then called Jeb and said

I'd overnight in Miami, en route to Brazil. He kindly invited me to stay the night, playing soccer with his young son and chatting with his wife, Columba, about Latin art. He wrote another letter to White House personnel staff, copying me, so I left with a glimmer of hope to begin the new year.

CHAPTER 7

Washington, DC (Bush I)

BEFORE LEAVING, I faxed Andy, the new deputy chief of staff, asking if he remembered me and would receive my visit. He responded that he remembered us standing on Boston's street corners in 1980, holding signs supporting George H. W. Bush for president. Another friend, Sheldon, who used to work in Rio's US consulate, agreed to house me while running the gauntlet of political employ inside DC.

Taking another leap of faith, I purchased a cheap ticket on Paraguayan Air, eventually landing at National (Reagan) Airport under snow. I found Sheldon's condo in Adams Morgan, in this transitional neighborhood, bustling with Latinos, Ethiopians, and urban pioneers. Near Columbia Road, where check-cashing joints mixed with trendy bistros, his condo would become my DC command post.

For someone without national profile, seeking political appointment became a daunting marathon. People within the Beltway maintained influence on the political process, and as insiders, they held the advantage to secure political appointments. A lobbyist once described the Beltway scenario as Republicans on one side and Democrats on the other, swooping down like vultures on capitol spoils. The process was presided by the grand-prize winner, the president of the United States.

Step one was to reconnoiter the "plum book," compiling political positions to be filled by incoming administrations. I noted a couple—one at the US Treasury, the deputy assistant secretary (DAS) of international institutions, and another at the US Information Agency as director of Television and Film Service. After several attempts, I secured an appointment with the Deputy Chief of Staff, giving my social, DOB, and street address in order to visit the West Wing.

Andy appeared exultant and raised his hands, saying, "What do you think?" He told me that that his brother-in-law was the Deputy of White House personnel—would I like to see him? He picked up the phone, securing an appointment with Ron, a Beltway insider, who asked, "Your Bush credentials look good: What position do you want to make a run for?"

"I've spent five years in show business, so probably the opening at USIA's TV and Film Service," I replied.

Ron nodded and counseled, "Whatever position you seek, remember to marshal your forces. Your competitors will. Whoever marshals the most support will win."

"Should I seek elected representatives to help my cause? I'm outside the Beltway, without many friends," I observed, fearing how I might fare.

"Make new friends. Call anyone willing to give you the time of day," he advised. "Calls are important," he added and sent me on my way.

His words ringing in my ear, I sought appointments with administrative assistants (AAs) of US Senator Gorton of Washington. Though a Republican in a Democratic Senate, he possessed clout on the important finance committee. I met with AAs Mike and Anthony, who secured five minutes to meet and greet the senator. They offered help, adding that I had one good shot for the senator to write or call in my behalf. They secured time with respected Congresswoman Dunn, who said she'd help too, once I'd declared for a post.

"Call everyone you know, and ask them to call in your behalf. The selection process is hit or miss, but the more calls the better," advised Bruce, a former counselor for Reagan, adding, "Lobbyists are important as well as think tanks like Heritage, AEI, and Cato in the incoming administration."

A week passed, and no one called. I rang Ron's assistant, asking if anything was set up. "Not yet at USIA," she said. "Possibly at Treasury. Would you be interested? "

I replied affirmatively, meeting two days later with the confirmed assistant secretary of International Affairs. Charles struck me as a scholarly type, asking conceptual questions about bank and finance experience south of the border. We had a stimulating twenty-minute talk in which I buttressed credentials at BankBoston and surviving Brazil's galloping inflation. Charles went on to become a major player in Wall Street, but at that time, he chose someone else for his DAS.

"Time to move on," I said, hoping rejection wouldn't keep me down.

Another week went by. Ron's assistant finally called and fixed an appointment with the newly confirmed director of the US Information Agency. I studied up on the director, who'd worked as VP of public relations for a major pharmaceutical firm in New York. His brother served as CEO and had been a big donor to the president's campaign. I reviewed the firm's annual report and noted substantial operations in Latin America and mentally mapped out my strategy.

On D-day at USIA, I was told that I'd have fifteen minutes and to make the most of it. The director seemed pleasant and asked why I deserved the job.

"I persevere under adverse circumstances," I said. "I could be your ally at USIA," mentioning starting up ten video operations for Paramount and Universal against tough odds in Latin America.

He seemed impressed that I "successfully navigated dicey Brazil," asking, "How would you advance America's public diplomacy overseas?"

"I'd build coalitions abroad in behalf of US initiatives using satellite TV. In Latin America, we joined attorneys, producers, and consumers to promote intellectual property against video pirates. We regained the marketplace and could do so again for the USA," I affirmed.

"As you're an outsider, how would you deal with government bureaucracy?" he inquired.

"I'd also build coalitions in America and seek support from public TV stations. They produce excellent documentaries and could tell America's story abroad," I replied, seeing his head nod twice.

He asked about Bush connections, happy to learn I'd supported the president in 1980 and counted Jeb as my friend. His assistant poked her head in at fifteen minutes, but the director went on for another ten. He thanked me for coming, and his assistant smiled on the way out.

That night, I debriefed with Sheldon, now working at USIA's educational bureau. To land this post, I'd need the director's support and that of White House personnel. The next day, I started marshaling my forces and asked Senator Gorton's AAs for him to write a letter and make a call. I also asked Jeb and Congresswoman Dunn to do likewise, and I called Fritz at the MPAA to strategize over lunch.

We shared news on studio personalities and MPAA priorities in DC—especially protection of intellectual property. He offered another five minutes with Jack to restate my case and to ask him to make the call. I did so and gave Fritz a brief list of talking points. Later, the political liaison officer informed me that Jack's call had "made the difference" for this highly sought political plum. Despite ties to LBJ and the Democratic Party, Jack had a bigger than life personality with a powerful PR machine. Politicos and appointees from either party sought to curry his favor, gaining invites to parties mentioned in *The Washington Post*'s society page.

After seven weeks of running the gauntlet, USIA's liaison officer called saying, "things looked good." She said I'd undergo an FBI background check when friends and associates would be interviewed. If nothing untoward was found, I'd be officially advised of selection in two months' time. I shared tentative news with supporters, thanking them for their help. Sheldon seemed relieved to see me going, and I flew to Rio feeling good.

As Brazil's summer waned, I started saying good-byes to friends. James hosted pleasant lunches at his condo overlooking Copacabana's vast beach. To arrive, however, I twice dodged thieves with knives. Rio was getting rougher—even my home was burglarized—another sign that it was time to leave.

In São Paulo, I bid *ciao* to Marques and Marcos—thriving at CIC Video—inviting them to DC. Back in Rio, Harry heard through the grapevine that my appointment was a sure bet, as long as "I minded my p's and q's and didn't cause embarrassment." I did my best to keep in check and lined up a tentative renter, just in case. Severina of Salgueiro prepared her special codfish lunch for Holy Week, hugging her American son who was packing his bags again. USIA faxed me that FBI background check was A-OK and to report for duty May 1.

Washington, DC, seemed delightful in May, with budding trees and blossoms. Yet in capitol corridors or along K Street, young staffers juggled their politico's agendas among lobbyists seeking an edge. I returned to Adams Morgan and found a sublet on Sixteenth Avenue NW, offering views of the White House. The apartment was furnished, so with my limited effects, that proved ideal.

Entering USIA's senior staff meeting, I looked younger than most, feeling a bit out of place. Around the table, chaired by the director, sat regional heads from Asia, Africa, the Americas, and Europe, as well as bureau heads of education, programs, Voice of America (VOA), and the TV service. The director's deputy, a holdover from the Reagan administration, served as the hammer and sat to the side with other staff like general counsel, congressional relations, and private sector. Each person reported on his or her respective area and tried to look good. I did my best, trying to firm up my voice.

The TV and Film Service was created by former USIA director Wicks, who had Hollywood ties. In 1983—the same year as CNN's founding—Worldnet was created to tell America's story abroad via satellite TV. Our main task was producing interactive teleconferences with US policymakers, like the secretary of state, connecting them with news organizations overseas. The teleconferences lasted two hours daily, so we filled remaining hours with C-Span to international audiences.

Our studios were removed from USIA, located north of the National Mall. As Worldnet was without a director, the deputy basically ran the three-hundred-person organization with little supervision. All six senior executives were Anglos over sixty-years old, without diversity in background or views. When I arrived, some friction ensued as the deputy was skeptical to change the pace of USIA's satellite TV organization.

Trying not to micromanage interactive programs, as they'd produced them for years, I focused on new programming for the twenty-two hours filled by C-Span. I assembled our private sector team, chaired by my former HBS roommate, Frank, with executives from the Black Entertainment Network, Univision, and PBS International. Thanks to these shakers and movers, we obtained programming for "noncommercial markets" in Eastern Europe, Africa, and Latin America, retransmitting the programming over satellite TV. My deputy seemed skeptical, but USIA's director seemed pleased.

That fall, the director tasked me to visit the USSR and Eastern Europe as President Bush encouraged more freedom of expression. Organizationally, USIA was an independent agency at the time, with a dotted line through secretary of state James Baker III, a major power broker. USIA served as the administration's PR agency abroad, advancing public policy set by the president and State Department.

To set up trip appointments, I worked through public affairs officers (PAO) of US embassies in Warsaw, Prague, Budapest, and Moscow—and with the station PAO in West Berlin. Below are vignettes from that memorable trip:

- *Checkpoint Charlie*: We crossed from West Berlin to the grayer East, entering a dimly lit tavern in a smoke-filled room. We joined a long table, conversing in German over bratwurst. This older resident from Saxony said, "Why shouldn't we break bread with

Westerners. What's wrong with this? We've had such a good conversation. *Auf wiedersehen.*"

- *Prague, Wenceslaus Square at night*: I heard rock 'n' roll upstairs and entered a makeshift disco with strobe lights and youngsters doing the twist. I spoke to a *svelte* Czech who cooed over pop music. I asked what her parents thought. "My father is *apparatchik* in the education ministry and would die if he knew." She smiled, moving in rhythm to Stevie Wonder.
- *Warsaw to Poznan by train*: An upstart Pole said he didn't join the Party, so he left to Switzerland, where he swept floors in a restaurant. He saved and planted strawberries in Poznan "with my money, my family, my work" and exported them to Zurich. "I'm now the strawberry king," he exulted, "with *dacha* and BMW. The state be damned."

I returned to DC and briefed the director. He was happy to learn of new, privately run TV stations in Poland and Hungary and encouraged our satellite feeds. We secured more no-charge programming from PBS superstations in Boston, Los Angeles, Pittsburg and Seattle, retransmitting to Eastern Europe.

Then Tiananmen Square protests broke out, with the lone student facing down the tanks. As directed by the secretary of state, we sent Voice of America programming in Mandarin on our Asia satellite, despite jamming by the PRC. We watched the harsh crackdown on CNN but saw the Berlin Wall crumble on New Year's Eve. Though new to the Beltway, I felt upbeat at USIA. We'd done our part in behalf of freedom as 1989 wound down.

Socially, the Capitol was vibrant around the holidays as lobbyists provided celebratory fuel. The MPAA soiree drew Hollywood stars and good ole boys, putting back caviar and champagne. Political appointees, like the VOA director, enjoying largesse from a wealthy spouse, catered dozens of politicos and lobbyists in their swank Georgetown townhouses.

We political appointees were invited to the White House at Christmas, and we waited in line to shake hands with patient president and Mrs. Bush, gaining signed photos as souvenirs. The New Year's Eve fireworks were stunningly patriotic in red, white, and blue, announcing the new world order in Washington, DC.

As newcomer to the DC scene, I learned of different social circles in which to play—with well-heeled lobbyists, power-driven politicos, or subtle diplomats. Each group sought influence over policy in its own way, wining and dining accessible political appointees to gain access. By virtue of my position, I received invitations to embassies for Independence Day celebrations, including for the arrival of tall ships from Oman. Moreover, Jeb's wife, Columba, was a devotee of Latin American art, gaining entrée to cultural attaches in embassies and multilateral agencies. Entertaining in DC remained key.

Socially, my small niche was to host monthly tea parties in my apartment on Sunday afternoons. I celebrated visitors like my mom, Aunt Maxine, or Brazilians escaping Carnaval. With a potpourri of attendees, we shared late news, catching quick glances of the White House and Capitol from my bay windows. Students from my Howard University course also showed up to check out the prof's digs.

Organizationally, two "guerilla" movements were stirring, creating a risk for my comfortable domain. First, came a quiet rebellion by older senior executives against my initiative for outside programming in their bailiwick. One person was particularly irksome, receiving critiques from female employees for keeping score on who helped or hindered his agenda inside. The US Civil Service rules proved burdensome to move him aside, taking sixteen months to organizationally isolate him without employees.

Alone inside his box, he continued to fume—especially upon my appointing the first female senior executive in his place. He alleged age discrimination to prevent the move. It required perseverance to deal with his countermoves, and I felt modestly successful, while still in charge.

The more threatening action came from the powerful associate director of the VOA, with his friends on K Street. Word was out that he coveted Worldnet, wanting TV to report to him rather than to USIA's director. To this novice of intra-agency politics, it was no contest, and in my third year in office, the VOA director had his way—the TV and Film Service reported to him.

He asked me to wait downstairs for his visit to Worldnet studios. Blustery wind blew snow that day, so I waited inside. A black Galaxy arrived at 10:00 a.m., its engine running outside our building. After ten minutes, the car was still there, so I wondered if that was he or someone else inside. I exited into the cold, seeing him in the back seat. He waited for me to open the door, impressing the point that he was boss and that I was subservient to him.

I opened the door, gritting my teeth. I remembered how power was DC's currency, not gentlemanly spirit, as taught at home. However, if cameras were rolling, smiles and nice words abounded. Yet when cameras were off, darker human behavior prevailed in corridors of power.

Another change descended on the agency, as the director secured an appointment as an ambassador in Europe, and a new Texan was named in replacement. After Senate confirmation of both appointments, I heard the new director had ideas for Worldnet TV. I tried to be accommodating but sensed he wanted his own person in charge, which happened by year's end. He offered me a face-saving appointment as senior advisor of Voice of America to expand USIA reach to cable TV in Latin America and Central Europe. USIA sent out a slick release on my new appointment, reported in the *Washington Post* that I was a "man on the move."

I hid my disappointment by hitting disco circuits and extending my nightlife. I attended Mass sporadically at St. Augustine's for its ten-thirty gospel service. Founded after the Civil War for African American Catholics, this tall Gothic church on Fifteenth and V had cache in DC's black community. I enjoyed meeting longstanding DC residents at coffee·hours—a pleasant change from DC's transience. The Monsignor confessed that I was the only Republican he knew who came to his Mass, inviting me to chat whenever I felt the need. I thanked him for his invite, tucking it away for another day.

My mother used to say that bad things happened in three's. Early 1992, my dear friend and former assistant at BankBoston, Dottie, passed away from cancer. I went to her memorial in Boston and felt sad for my loyal friend, passing early in life.

Later in March, I was tapped to attend an international telecommunication forum in Toledo, Spain, on behalf of VOA and Worldnet. It was a delightful conference in the Alcazar, with pleasant tours and luncheons with European executives and broadcast owners. The leisurely week continued to Madrid with visits to TV stations and late dinners along the Gran Via. I returned to DC, feeling good, and reported back to VOA about upbeat meetings.

On my birthday that month, I arrived home late and heard my mother's message on my answering machine, wishing me a happy birthday. I called her back the next day but heard a weakened voice on the line. Later that week, I arrived to work before 9:00 a.m. and received the call from my sister, who said that my mom had just passed away. She had died of internal bleeding in Pamela's arms. My sister, called 911, and an ambulance arrived quickly—but to no avail. Mom had passed from this world.

I hung up in shock and began to sob uncontrollably, descending VOA's backstairs past surprised colleagues. I left the building in a fog, wandering around in the cold. I found an open church door and sat in the back pew, unable to hide my tears. I began to pray but was overpowered by grief. I wondered how I'd cope with life.

My mother was my anchor in this world—the person I'd always tried to please. She'd always accepted me in good times and in bad, and she extolled my virtues to friends and family. Now she was no longer among the living—unable to say good-bye. That thought shook me to the core, and sadness flowed unchecked. I didn't return to the VOA; rather, I sought out the Monsignor who, with dignity, heard me out. He put his hand on my shoulder and offered a prayer for my mother's soul and for my own, transfigured in pain. He said that he'd pray for me every day until my return and that I should go home soon.

My brother flew home from Muscat, where he taught chemistry at Oman's Sultan Qaboos University. We met at the funeral home, where my mother's body was kept cold. Her face looked drawn, without life. My brother reminded how her body was the vessel for her living spirit, which had been lifted to a better place. Tears rolled down our cheeks as we bade our mother good-bye, even though her spirit had left her. We remembered her in our own ways and exited into light rain. I noticed azaleas blooming, Mom's favorite flower of the spring.

We planned her memorial at University Lutheran, where Dad was honored twelve years before. The church overflowed with friends and family, paying tribute to this kind lady we called Mom. Testimonies of her thoughtfulness and of being a good neighbor were abundant; a special tribute in poem was read by cousin Pat. I remembered our father's words that a measure of a person's worth came at life's end, when people came to honor the deceased for the impact she'd had on them.

Pamela was Mom's executor and followed her will to divide the modest estate. We went through memorabilia and old correspondence at our family home in Laurelhurst amid tears and nostalgia. In a few days, we'd sorted out mementos as we recalled special times with Mom. Our time proved cathartic and helped us bond more closely. We gave each other extended hugs as Terry and I departed to separate corners of the world. My sister was stalwart in holding down the fort and prepared its sale. As I flew east, I asked myself: If I returned to Seattle, where would I stay?

Back in DC, I lost motivation to keep up appearances, important in daily political life. My center of gravity had been altered, unsure as to where it'd be. Some asked me to get involved with the president's reelection campaign, but I declined—my energy was no longer there. I moped around and wondered what I'd do if the president didn't prevail. Some USIA colleagues had left early, working for lobbyists on K Street. Did I really want to go that route? Was that to be my life's raison d'etre?

I'd witnessed the pursuit of power up close, impacting people's lives, not all for good. Most people in DC seemed consumed with power, so removed from the rest of the country. While sorting out those issues and grieving my mom's passing, I returned to Rio for modest business but more for R & R. I swam in the Atlantic, walked Copa's beach, and revisited old friends, trying to heal.

Returning via Miami, in Hurricane Andrew's aftermath, I wondered about living there, where Jeb had his home. Should I seek my way in the Crossroads of the Americas, speaking English or *español?*

Turning Point: Accept a Position in a Trade Association for a Six-Figure Salary, or Move to Miami Beach for Another Adventure to Unfold?

November, the president lost his reelection to the comeback kid, as did yours truly—losing his position at USIA. I was joined by two thousand GOP appointees, all bailing ship and seeking positions inside the Beltway. As forecasted by my mother, I suffered my third loss in 1992 but prepared myself for another day.

CHAPTER 8
Miami Beach

MIAMI'S WARM BREEZE was welcoming that November, so different than DC's. Snowbirds bustled out of the plane, seeking refuge from the cold. I drove to South Beach, past art deco buildings, recalling scenes from *Scarface*. Along Ocean Drive, neon-lit discos and smart restaurants gave contrast to the beach's older look. Crowds of young Latinos and Anglos flocked the streets, and I felt as loose as a goose in trendy Sobe.

I camped out a week at the hostel on Washington Avenue, seeking a new place to call home. I checked out art deco offerings and was tempted to rent. A Canadian at the hostel suggested looking along West Avenue, away from the zoo. At the South Bay Club on Eighth Street, I checked in and met Pat, a resident realtor. She showed me condos to buy or to rent, belatedly showing me a two-bedroom unit above her flat. I closed on that condo on the club's third floor, admiring cruise ships transiting Biscayne Bay.

Greater Miami was called the Crossroads of the Americas with good reason. I met several Brazilians, Canadians, Venezuelans, and Colombians—some European tourists too. The Cuban community ran the city of Miami, but older Jewish citizens influenced beach politics. Both communities seemed to get along, though not all Latinos with the dominant *cubanos*. All were working to make new lives in Dade County, seeking their version of the American dream. Through friends of friends, I made new acquaintances and felt hopeful to begin a new home.

Thanks to Jeb's entrée to the Beacon Council, I met several in the business and banking communities. Roger, a friend from Rio, worked for a shipping company, giving me heads up on business dealings with fly-by-night artists. We often lunched at Versailles on Calle Ocho, savoring Ropa Vieja or Cuban pork sandwiches, with a *café cubano* to top it off. I continued knocking on doors of smaller firms with an eye to Latin America but found competition fierce as another consultant.

At a chamber luncheon, I met bankers from Goldman Sachs who recommended me as a mentor to Cities in Schools. They assigned me two boys named Danny at a charter school—one of Puerto Rican parents and another with Cuban roots. Mentors met weekly with students, helping academically but also sharing life skills. Our goal was to support students toward graduation, despite challenges at home. The Dannys often invited me to family dinner around holidays, feasting on succulent roast pig. A few years later, we celebrated their walks down the aisle, as they went forth in life.

Besides mentoring, I secured part-time consulting but generally had time on my hands. My daily routine was to jog down West Avenue until the island's southern point and then along Ocean Drive and finally to a rewarding *café cubano*. I'd frequent libraries in Miami Beach or Coral Gables to do research on local firms—setting up visits afterward. I met with friends from my Bush or BankBoston days, renewing our relationship while raising my flag. Friends like Herb of La Cubanísima, or Gene from Brazil, provided insights to Cuban American politics, strongly opposed to Castro's regime.

After such meetings, I'd hope to connect over lunch, perhaps at Versailles or, if alone, at cafeterias serving Cuban or Brazilian cuisine. From Thursday through Sunday, I'd check out discos along Ocean Drive or Lincoln Mall, learning some salsa during nocturnal forays.

Visitors started arriving my second winter, when temperatures were pleasant and ocean breezes fair. UW friends like Keith and Alison visited from Seattle, the Murphy clan from Oman, and snowbirds from DC or Boston seeking respite. It was fun showing off my new environs, yet I yearned for permanent work in a city of short stints. Cities in Schools gave kudos on both Dannys' graduation, inquiring if I'd like to mentor again in the inner city. I said yes.

My consulting MO was to pitch expertise in countries like Brazil and the Dominican Republic, where Miami firms sought licensees or venture partners. Considered a permanent resident in Brazil, I travelled there yearly and proposed sharing expenses with prospective clients to make it worthwhile. On the political front, Jeb intimated interest to run for governor in 1994, against an incumbent who'd served two terms. It looked like a dogfight in this toss up state, but I signed on early to help his campaign.

That fall, I began mentoring new students at Miami Jackson, where dealers and gangs roamed outside. I came to know classmates within a special academy that focused on personal responsibility and military discipline. Learning of my business background, the mentoring chair asked if I'd share insights in personal finance.

So began my tour as volunteer teacher of economics at Jackson High School. Some students spoke about starting up businesses, explaining how they'd find customers for a new beauty salon. Others debated how much they'd pay fellow workers: even classmates demanded more than minimum wage. We always had stirring debates with students engaged. I felt inspired as they dreamed big, receiving *mucho* satisfaction if not income.

I meandered along that year, with small-time gigs at small-time firms. At a conference on Latin America, I met more promising company executives, including PR Newswire's regional VP. They offered steady but part-time work at its Coral Gables headquarters to map strategy south of the border. PRN encouraged Latin American firms to relist shares on US stock exchanges so that American investors could purchase stateside. Again, as data was limited in pre-Google days, its niche was to raise international firms' profiles to investors willing to take a chance in shares.

Jeb declared his candidacy for governor early in 1994 and began ramping up the campaign—especially in home Dade County. As I'd been in touch with small business groups, I worked in that area, while Jeb flushed out his staff. Typical of most media, Florida's reporting favored left-of-center candidates. Thus, Jeb battled this bias by engaging journalists one-on-one, often with positive results. He highlighted plans to raise the quality and accountability of public education, showing willingness to meet communities of all races and walks of life. He epitomized for me the type of Republicans I've supported throughout my life.

On the personal front, I continued my wander, enjoying the South Beach nightlife, or so I thought. Despite trendy clubs and pleasant temperatures by day, I felt I was marking time without distinction or direction. The most uplifting time continued in class at Miami Jackson, with inner city kids, providing purpose and spark. The academy's discipline offered both of us structure as we pursued daily life. Spiritually, however, my life drifted out like a receding tide. I wondered if another wave might bring me back to a more hopeful place.

Pleasant spring turned into scorching summer. I turned up my AC to escape from 90 percent humidity and ninety-degrees days. Summer storms were spectacular as thunder and lightning rolled in. When hurricane season arrived, I became restless, watching The Weather Channel with care. For those who hadn't experienced a hurricane threat, it proved scary. TV trackers counted down the storm's approach and viewers ran to the malls. Often, fights broke out among shoppers battling over scarce water, plywood, or canned food. I'd hear neighbors boarding up windows, fearful of the incoming storm.

Amigo Giora offered refuge in his Doral Estates home to residents like me, exposed on the Beach. We hunkered down in his basement as high winds raced overhead. Fortunately for us in Miami, Hurricane Gordon veered northward instead.

Jeb's campaign kicked into higher gear, and the race tightened up. Several newspapers endorsed him, and 1994 seemed like a GOP year. With Bill Clinton facing scandal and Newt boasting a contract for America, trends seemed hopeful. Besides outreach to small businesses, my Cuban American friend Osvaldo and I also rang doorbells in Hispanic neighborhoods in English and *en español*.

Yet Jeb's election was not to be, losing the closest gubernatorial race in Florida's history by sixty-four thousand votes. Despite campaign rancor and disappointment, Jeb congratulated his opponent with grace and aplomb. He was elected governor in 1998 and reelected in 2002 by six hundred and fifty thousand votes. Most Anglo and Latino votes said yes and awarded him their highest public opinion as his term came to an end.

* * *

Turning Point: A Spiritual Odyssey

Later in January, my friends Eric of Goldman Sachs and Joe of FCA invited me to the NFL's Super Bowl breakfast, held at the Omni Hotel on Biscayne Boulevard. This was my first prayer breakfast to attend, not knowing what to expect. Young athletes and professionals in coat and tie sat around tables, eager to hear from NFL athletes. Athletes in Action was the sponsor, along with businesses like Goldman.

The program included athletes' testimonies about how they'd come to faith. Redskins coach Joe Gibbs asked, "In the game of life, God is our coach. But are we playing on his team?" In 1995, Chris Carter from the Minnesota Vikings received the NFL's Bart Starr award "for character and leadership," saying, "My hundred and twenty-two catches are so small by comparison to my relationship with Jesus Christ. He loved me when I didn't love myself. He had faith in me when I had none. He listened to me while others turned their backs. How can I thank him or be worthy of his love?"

His words electrified the room. As the lights turned on, I was one of two thousand damp-eyed professionals but wondered on whose team I was playing? A clarion sounded deep inside, reminding me of my spirit, so overtaken by the material world. Pondering the athletes' words, I left unsettled and drove toward Coral Gables Library.

Across Sevilla Avenue, a tall-steepled church loomed, so I stopped to see if I could just pray. The attendant pointed me to a darkened chapel where I stumbled through the Lord's Prayer. I crossed back to the library, where I usually did corporate research. The librarian looked quizzically as I asked for a Bible instead of the *Standard & Poor's*. I began reading the book of John, feeling as if the words leapt off the page, reaching its zenith in John 3:16. This day seemed special—was it a sign? I decided it was time to begin my own spiritual odyssey, rather than seeking pleasure out and about.

The following Sunday, I attended St. Louis Catholic parish in South Miami and felt moved when its lights darkened for the consecration of the bread and wine. It'd been a while since taking communion, so in silence, I asked the Lord's forgiveness on the come. I felt better that Sunday but backslid the following week when temptations took hold. I sought other churches around Miami, receiving an invite from a student to attend his African American Baptist church.

The pastor's words rang out strongly at the altar call: "The Lord doesn't care what burdens you carry, what lifestyle you've led, or what race you might be." Looking at me, he continued, "Ask His forgiveness, and start a life of Spirit. Come forth in the name of Christ." Wanting to stand up, but lacking confidence to profess faith, I slid down in the pew. Yet the pastor exhorted, "Don't let the evil one keep you seated—stand up for Jesus!"

I was terrified and felt the Holy Spirit's laser on me. I ran out of church that morning, not wanting to face that pastor or his gospel-singing congregation. "What's happening?" I asked. "Why's God stalking me?" In my South Beach condominium, I watched the sun set over Biscayne Bay. I turned the TV to CBS for *60 Minutes*, but found March Madness instead. I flipped channels and landed on David Robinson, giving his testimony on ABC.

Then cameras scanned to San Juan's stadium, where Billy Graham preached in English with a Puerto Rican priest translating *en español*. Their words touched me, as had the NFL athletes, the Baptist pastor, and David Robinson's testimony. Reverend Graham confirmed how everyone had a purpose in life. It was up to us to discover our own, even with doubts. He noted how Moses was unsure about his but asked Yahweh, in whose name was he to lead the Jewish people to the Promised Land?

"God responded, 'I am that I am; *yo soy que yo soy.*' That is what you are to say to the Israelites. *I am* has sent me to you."

That very morning, I'd read that Bible passage found in Exodus 3:14! How could this be mere coincidence? "Alone" in my living room, without distractions or excuses, fifty years of tears surged over my dam of pride and self-doubt. I took that leap of faith and prostrated myself. I asked the Lord's forgiveness of my sins and broken promises. I asked him to accept me as his son.

My brother, Terry, called from Muscat the next day to wish me a happy birthday in family tradition. I shared my spiritual journey and confessed becoming his brother in faith. We wept. Cousin Pat later asked how I felt. I said, "Lighter—as life's burdens had left my shoulders, given up to Jesus Christ." My concerns of being successful paled in importance as I sought my unique destiny, guided by him. I prayed for his signs rather than following my whims. The center of gravity in my life had changed. And interesting events began coming in.

Earlier, the tequila effect of Mexico's devaluation affected many Latin American economies. As a consultant, my phone did not ring. Later that month, PR Newswire's Pat asked me to chair a panel on business opportunities in Latin America. PRN's president was in the audience. On conclusion, he asked me to head a project to enlist Latin American exchanges to use PR's online news services.

They approved travel to São Paulo, where I paid a courtesy visit to the US consul general. As we wound down our meeting, he asked if I'd like to assist a Brazilian TV group to find strategic alliances abroad. I affirmed that I would and met with TV Bandeirantes's CEO, Johnny, and concluded another contract in less than a month. We'd met during Paramount Pictures and USIA days, maintaining a positive dialogue. How this consulting business came about, I cannot say. Yet Brazilians told me that "it had fallen from heaven," so I praised the Lord.

My teaching continued at Miami Jackson, where we began a game of the stock market, an alien creature to most students. Some thought the market was where cattle were slaughtered, and I smiled saying that sometimes "bulls" had been. Each student chose a publicly traded company, with which they had connection—McDonalds, Burger King, Home Depot, AT&T, Telemundo. 1995 was a good year for the kids from Jackson High whose portfolio beat the *S&P* 500, as later recognized in the *Wall Street Journal's* editorial.

Later quoted in the *Miami Herald* article "Saluting Volunteers: He Makes At-Risk Kids His Business," the high school's academy director, Larry remarked, "They might scream at him…but nothing deters him in his zeal to help these kids." Said student Tory, "It's fun. He's teaching us something we never thought about learning. It keeps me interested because I'm competing with other students."

To that same church, where I'd tried to say the Lord's Prayer earlier that year, we returned Christmas Eve. University Baptist Church emphasized creative dramatics in its services, much appreciated by the kids. We'd attended UBC on other Saturday evenings, adjourning later to an all-you-could-eat Chinese buffet along the Miracle Mile. We gave thanks for the reason for the season over this heavenly banquet and wished each other *Feliz Navidad.*

* * *

Despite positive happenings in Miami, I yearned to return to Seattle. While daily life was pleasant and my faith reborn, Miami Beach didn't feel like home. I read interviews by reporters asking where people were from, with responses like Cuba, Nicaragua, Venezuela, New York, or Ohio. Few mentioned Miami, even those with long residence. Maybe they felt so because of South Florida's transience—I could only surmise.

TV Bandeirantes continued to engage me to connect with entertainment firms abroad. When we next met in São Paulo, I pleaded my case to return to Seattle. Johnny looked at me and then to the map. Miami and New York were cities most visited by Brazilians, but the West Coast not so. He finally nodded and broke into a smile: "*Tudo bem*, Estive. As long as you'll be where and when we want you, then move back to your beloved homeland. Who knows? I may visit you."

I thanked him. "*Obrigado*, Johnny!"

Later, I'd hoped to visit my hometown, wondering where I'd stay. My longtime amigo Donaldo welcomed me to his Mountlake home, sensing a difficult transition without Mom. It was fun getting to know his lively family and reconnoitering Seattle, changing as it had while I lived away. My second cousin Marilee in Portland learned of my return, asking if her number-two son, Austin, might join my cross-country trek. He'd also bring my favorite "Voodoo donut" from the City of Roses, created by another entrepreneurial second cousin, Tres.

The Jackson students were told of my Seattle intentions and became sad. They gave me a two-foot "thank you card," signed by academy students, still kept in my room today. While I'd hoped to impart knowledge of economics, they'd boosted me with purpose during tough days without work. I still maintain contact with many, including Richard, who helped design this book. Thank you, students of Miami Jackson High School—you are the best!

Austin arrived in June, visiting his dad's family and attending UBC's Bible camp for teens. Afterward, we bid good-bye to UBC friends and packed up household goods on a fourteen-foot U-Haul truck. We departed Miami beneath a tropical storm but made it to Atlanta by the Fourth of July, overnighting with Peruvian friends. We crossed Alabama to Tennessee, where my nephew found a fireworks supermarket, buying Roman candles and four-foot firecrackers as presents for his family back in Portland: "Do you think they'll like them, Uncle Steve?"

We continued north by northwest and reached Montana. To my fifteen-year-old nephew's chagrin, Uncle Steve hadn't let him drive the truck. He stopped talking for a day. We reached a truce of sorts, when I agreed to let him take the wheel, once crossing the border to the Evergreen State.

On The Edge

We reached Othello on I-90, seeing a long, straight road ahead. I finally relented and gave Austin his turn. He did so with diligence, reaching the Cascade foothills safe and sound. After this long trip across brown steppes and deserts, we felt joy in seeing green. We gave thanks for those Douglas fir trees in the Pacific Northwest and gleefully sped down the highway, home at last.

CHAPTER 9

A Different Seattle

WE'D GROWN UP in Seattle as a blue-collar town, with Boeing as our corporate big brother. Many aspired for a job on its assembly line for 707, 727, 737, or 747 airplanes. Weyerhaeuser and pulp mills had traditional roots in the Evergreen State, and Nordstrom was slowly expanding beyond the Pacific Northwest. Neighbors always helped neighbors and rebelled when downtown interests overstepped their bounds. My dad and fellow citizens rallied to save the Pike Street market to world renown.

Things from the East were held in low esteem, and Seattleites voted down the metro in the sixties as an unwanted import from the big city. This was my hometown upon UW graduation in 1966, before I began my odyssey East and to Vietnam and south of the border. At college, we had but one Mexican restaurant in the University District but several taverns a mile from campus. We had the blue laws then.

In the late nineties, Microsoft had completed two decades, creating IT employment and a lifestyle change. Starbucks was expanding, spurring competitors like Ladros and Tully's to satisfy our espresso demand. Fine restaurants like Wild Ginger enticed a demanding clientele, and chefs around the world brought fusion cuisine. French wineries discovered the Yakima Valley, exporting wine to international acclaim. This was the "hometown" I'd found thirty years later.

Raised in Northeast Seattle, I gravitated back, staying with Aunt Lucy in her Hawthorne Hills flat. I reconnected with Fr. Joy of Blessed

Sacrament who welcomed me as prodigal son. We'd often attend University Presbyterian's youth services Sunday nights with other Catholic friends. We admired Pastor Earl's sermons, whose academic brilliance and humor helped drive his message home. We'd adjourn to international bistros on "the Ave," conversing how to stay on track. He recommended joining fellowship groups to keep faith in sync, like Teleios Bible Study in over sixty Seattle-area homes.

To elevate my Latin American profile to Seattle's business community, *Puget Sound Business Journal* asked me to pen an article on opportunities south of the border. That article stimulated inquiries and a call from Seattle University, asking if I'd teach a class called Doing Business in Latin America. I concurred and began part-time teaching at SU's Albers School these past twenty years. We divided class into Latin America's five largest economies, each country reporting weekly on current events. Guest speakers shared real experiences and evaluated student proposals for their country of choice. Presentations focused on Seattle-based firms, like PACCAR, Blue Nile, and Costco—with my namesake at Costco wowing class with sophisticated matrices overseas.

Given my recent leap of faith, I put it to work around the hometown. Blessed Sacrament's program for a Mexican orphanage sought godfathers and godmothers for kids. I joined them on mission, bonding with brothers Marcos and Manuel in Tecate's Rancho Nazareth. As their homes were influx, our role was to provide human encouragement and financial support. We'd also paint buildings and erect fence posts, hanging out with the kids and playing soccer of sorts. We stood with them at first communion and have kept in touch over the years.

Friends recommended me to mentor two students in Rainier Beach High School, where Junior Achievement tapped me to teach economics—mostly to Coach B's basketball team. Discipline proved challenging, but I persisted every week, trying to engage teenagers in personal finance, like credit cards and auto loans. Their favorite project was to inspect boutiques in Southcenter Mall, analyzing shops' business models and teen marketing appeal. Our students impressed—one got a job as an assistant and another as a model. Better yet, students made connections to concepts taught in class.

Yet all was not rosy, as some of the team proved disruptive. Once, I kept them after class, and they were not pleased. The six-foot-six forward called me out, saying, "Mr. Murphy, we got better things to do; why you keep us late?"

"Jason, econ may not register now, but it'll help you deal with all your money, inside or out of the NBA," I countered, earning some smiles.

"But you come through to us like black-and-white TV," he asserted, gaining smirks from fellow teammates.

But another player, the coach's son, spoke up: "But that's OK, Mr. Murphy. Because we know you care."

Maybe something was getting through, after all!

Later that year, we cheered Daryl and Joe at graduation, the first in their families to make the walk. I'd sometimes take them to UPC's youth services, where they sighed, looking bored. Fast-forward ten years—I ran into Daryl's mother at Southcenter, who said her son began attending church. I exclaimed, "Wow, how come?" She knew how we tried engaging him as a teenager without much luck.

His mom smiled broadly, affirming, "Daryl just said, 'It was time.'"

At SU, they asked me to coteach international benchmarking with Professors Karen and Harriet, planning a study mission to Brazil. We compared US production techniques with Brazilian counterparts and visited Boeing, PACCAR, Sheraton, and Redhook. In São Paulo and Rio, we inspected production lines at Mercedes, Embraer, GM, and Brahma Beer. Client Johnny hosted a reception high on TV Bandeirantes's tower in São Paulo, offering panoramic views and plenty of cheer. At SU's senior talk out at graduation, several students cited this mission as high point in school.

Professionally, I consulted in between classes, affiliating with Pacific Northwest Advisors to broaden my reach. Target clients were small to midsize firms of $5–$100 million in sales, seeking agents or licensees south of the border. My MO on trips was to enlist companies to divide my time and travel expense, and to meet friends of friends in trade associations to secure reliable leads.

Seattle was chosen to host the World Trade Organization's talks in 1999 in hopes for a "Seattle agreement" among 150 countries planning to attend. Seattle's host committee tapped me as liaison to the Omani delegation, as I'd twice visited Muscat, where Terry taught chemistry at Sultan Qaboos University. Omani hospitality was cordial, almost biblical in spirit, so I hoped Seattle would replicate such welcome. Hundreds arrived from around the world, expecting positive times and discussions. Little did we know that another menace lurked, stalking delegates in the Emerald City.

Anarchists around the country poured in to disrupt WTO's proceedings, forcing confrontation, broken windows, and general unrest. Trying to reach the convention center, I ran interference for the Omanis, dodging protesters' placards and anarchist stones. Businesses boarded up windows and tear gas wafted in the air. "Violence in Seattle" headlined the media.

Inside, delegate emotions were taut and negotiations on the brink. After days of wrangling in a backdrop of crisis, talks ended in impasse, another north-south divide. The Seattle round floundered the end of that year, and delegates escaped to their homelands, some vowing never to return.

In the aftermath, my laid-back city felt dazed, and Seattle's mayor did not survive reelection. I asked pardon to the Omani's for my hometown's disruption, but the world was changing, with international trade less secure. Yet I continued outreach abroad, hoping that dialogue would prevail over retrograde actions with the new millennium around the corner.

In Y2K, I continued missions abroad, the first to El Salvador. Organized by Agros and UW students, we laid home foundations in new faith-based communities and funded a new grade school. Despite my sore back, I participated in St. Bridget's elephant stampede to raise funds for our sister parish in Malawi. Under Deacon Denny's leadership, material support had increased. He encouraged parishioners to visit Namitembo over Christmas to inaugurate our good works.

Parishioner Louise and I left in December, reading about hanging chads in Florida, our presidential election in doubt. In line at Johannesburg's airport for our flight to Malawi, I ran into its interior minister who asked with a smile if his country could help out. Finally, the Supreme Court ruled as we arrived, but we avoided political talk with Fr. Owen, our welcoming host.

On Sunday, he consecrated bread and wine under a mango tree as parishioners sang and danced during two-hour Mass. He later guided us to smaller communities in his parish of one hundred thousand souls, dodging crocodiles and hippos in the river. His parishioners exemplified hospitality in their humble abodes, offering big smiles and, sometimes, their last egg.

"I feel ashamed, Father. How can I eat the last egg in the house?" I mumbled, looking down.

"They're honoring you, as visitors, with all that they have," he replied.

"But what can I give in return?"

"Give them your love," he advised. Then he added, "Tell others in Seattle about what you've witnessed in your sister parish. We are always grateful for support."

Though we inaugurated its new youth center, I felt inadequate compared to this village's generosity and example of humility. *Zikomo, Namitembo*—May our paths cross soon, and may your land be blessed by rain.

On return, an attorney friend asked if I'd consider becoming a Rotarian. I said that I'd never been asked, so Lee invited me to University Sunrise Rotary for breakfast. Thus, began my ties with Rotary, the largest service organization in the world, whose motto is "service above self." Our club sponsored international service projects and invited speakers weekly to keep us informed. The program chair was Vicki Gilfillan Daly, whose recently deceased husband was cofounder of this active club.

Lee and I encouraged Rotarians with a yen for Latin American cuisine to dine at local bistros. Vicki began attending these dinners, arriving at my home to caravan to Vuelve a la Vida, a Mexican seafood restaurant in Tacoma. That evening, however, other Rotarians didn't show, so we went there together, our first date "by chance." She remembered my singing "Cielito Lindo" over margaritas, courtesy of the owner, Señor Douglas. Afterward, as the sun was setting, we promenaded around Wapato Lake hand-in-hand. One Sunday, she joined me for Mass at St. Bridget's, when Denny announced RCIA classes would soon begin. This course instructed non-Catholics our tenets of faith and, on completion, confirmed new members in the Catholic Church. Vicki signed up!

In DC, I'd followed George W.'s transition as president. Andy became his chief of staff, though Cheney's role overshadowed the inner circle. Some former colleagues returned to the Bush fold, but the lure of DC didn't register anymore. Besides, I was seriously dating a delightful lady and spending quality time with Vicki.

The dean of DC's ambassadors, René, invited me on mission to El Salvador to provide relief and hope to its people who were suffering another earthquake. As we'd just been rattled in Seattle, the ambassador thought my going worthwhile, so I joined this delegation, led by Honorable Elizabeth Dole. We found devastation all 'round, including in Suchitoto, where we'd built foundations a year before. The Red Cross brought material relief, and we delegates brought a human touch, standing with the Salvadoran people at midyear. Returning home, I also visited briefly White House personnel.

In Seattle, my nephew Jason joined my little household in the U District, providing youthful exuberance and welcome company. My daily routine was to jog through Cowan-Ravenna Park, perhaps around Green Lake and then to teach a class at SU. Vicki and I continued seeing each other, inside and out of Rotary. I wondered if this was really happening in this phase of life. I kept on praying that this widowed lady was whom the Lord had in mind and slowly came to believe the *M*-word possible at fifty-seven years.

And then September 11 arrived. Jason said, "Uncle Steve, you should see what's happening in New York now," and we both watched in horror as the second tower came tumbling down. We were in shock like our neighbors and wondered what had happened to our country, so vulnerable then. That night, we took a break from the news and walked the neighborhood. We saw people kneeling on their lawns and joined them in the Lord's Prayer.

My own little action was to sign up for Arabic at the UW to possibly reach out to native speakers. I met students with similar mind-set, believing we should do something after 9/11, to bridge the gap between Muslims and the postmodern West. We read about wars on terror, asking where it would end. We followed the Afghan and Iraqi invasions—Hussein's statue toppling down—and hoped for the best.

Vicki and I attended Mass together, occasionally Sunday services at UPC, where an usher Lyle recruited us to pass the plate. We appreciated Pastor Earl's various courses on the Beatitudes and the Old Testament, feeling like we moved closer in sync. We spent Christmas at Vicki's home bedecked for the season and nourished hope in the new year.

On Groundhog's Day, we attended Mass at St. Bridget's, and I asked for the priest's blessing for what I was about to do. In my Saturn II, I took Vicki to Snoqualmie Falls Lodge for breakfast. In the small private room overlooking the falls, I knelt down, requesting her hand. And she said yes! The waitress glimpsed in, soon arriving with champagne to celebrate our engagement. We ate the hearty country breakfast, looking lovingly under filtered sunshine. We began attending premarital sessions at a UPC couple's home in Shoreline and took the Minnesota compatibility test. Despite different backgrounds, we tested "compatible," thanks to our common faith in God and our willingness to talk through issues.

In early April, I received a call from Roberto of the Peace Corps, asking if I'd be available to interview for the position of the regional director of the Inter-Americas and Pacific area. I inquired if it'd be on "your dime or mine," and he chuckled, saying the USG would take care of it. I flew to DC and met with Roberto, who introduced me to the new Peace Corps director and chief of staff (COS). They noted my experience in Bush I and saw letters from Jeb. They asked about my experience south of the border, and I mentioned recent missions to Mexico, El Salvador, and Brazil. The interview lasted for forty minutes, and they said they'd be in touch.

Returning home, Seattle U asked if I'd teach my mainstay course on Latin America that summer. I mentioned that I'd just interviewed the Peace Corps but would let them know mid-May. Friends at SU and returned Peace Corps volunteers (RPCV) encouraged me onward. SU's president, Stephen, wrote a letter of recommendation.

When I spoke with Vicki about that possibility, she responded, "Let's go!" The Peace Corps chief of staff called in mid-May asking me to consider a different position than Latin America, such as the private sector post. It took few seconds to say, "No, thank you." I responded diplomatically that I was not seeking a political posting this time, rather one in the region that I loved.

He thanked me for my time and hung up. I concluded, *Well, that's it*, so I returned to SU to renew my contract for the Latin America course. I was disappointed, yes, but I thought maybe it was for the best. As a newly engaged couple, we had to plan our wedding going forward. Getting married late in life would prove challenging enough, getting to know one another a high priority. Yet in the morning of May 26, the COS called again, asking if I were still interested in the regional director position. I thought for a couple of seconds, and asked when he needed reply. When he said, "In two days," I thanked him and said I'd call back.

Turning Point: To Stay Safe in Seattle and Plan for Marriage or Venture Again to DC for the Peace Corps?

Arriving at SU, I wondered what I'd say to the management chair, having renewed my contract ten days before. His assistant greeted instead, so I described my predicament. She clapped her hands, saying that I could do both the Peace Corps and SU. I was unsure, as the COS demanded total commitment to this high profile job. I left Pigott Hall and entered St. Ignatius Chapel, a quiet refuge on this urban campus. I sat in the pew and reflected on the leafless tree, letting my mind and spirit wander. I remembered the parable of the talents—how those with more talents would be expected to give more in life. To bury one's talents in a hole didn't work out too well.

That day, I'd scheduled lunch with John, who served as Washington State's international director, with Mexican roots. Over lunch in the U Village, he noted my concerned look, so I shared my quandary concerning the offer from the Peace Corps. "I'm not sure what to do, as I've committed to teach my Latin American course at SU," I confided.

"Steve, that's easy. I'll teach your course, and you take the job—it's tailor-made for you!" he exclaimed with gusto.

"Are you sure, John, as it may conflict with your busy schedule?"

"It'd be a pleasure, amigo. Go to DC, and do us good in Latin America," he confirmed.

I thanked him and checked with SU. They concurred. I spoke with Vicki, who said, sure, again. Finally, I called the COS and accepted his offer, asking when to report for duty. He said in a month.

That June was a rushed affair, deciding to sell my U-District home (to my chagrin) and prepare my abrupt move to DC again. Vicki was supportive but unsure how it'd affect our plans. I said that we'd continue steps to get married after this brief pause. My idea was to first get resettled, then marry and have Vicki move to our new DC residence. Fortunately, the house sold quickly, and Jason, Vicki, and I packed up my minimal household goods.

I gave a long hug to Vicki and said quick good-byes to friends and family. I pushed my Saturn II hard during its first cross-country trip, arriving for duty at Peace Corps under Bush II.

CHAPTER 10

Peace Corps (Bush II)

"Ask not what your country can do for you. Ask what you can do for your country," said JFK in his famous words at inauguration.

His words still resonated with me on the eve of my appointment as the Peace Corps regional director of the Inter-Americas and Pacific (IAP) region. In high school, I'd been an early booster, even writing a letter to the editor to the *Seattle Times* to counter Senator Goldwater's critique. PC Director Shriver even acknowledged with a letter of his own, pleasing my parents.

Though there were over a dozen political appointees in the Peace Corps, the organization was run by returned Peace Corps volunteers, passionate about PC goals, which I paraphrase:

- To meet host country needs for trained people
- To promote understanding of Americans among the peoples served
- To promote understanding of other peoples in America

The term of appointment for PC civil servants was two-and-a-half years, renewable for another term. This permitted personnel turnover unlike in other government agencies.

As I had served in the US Navy and was not an RPCV, I wondered if I'd be accepted by this organization known for its strong culture within.

My Saturn II reached RPCV Vivian and Fernando's home in Vienna, in time for quick greetings, including from the twin tabby cats under my care. On July 1, I took the metro to headquarters, finding the chief of staff in a reasonable mood. So far, so good, I thought. He introduced me to Maryann, who'd served as interim IAP director with longstanding PC credentials.

I learned that the IAP region was created in an earlier budget deal, putting together Latin American and Pacific-island countries in order to save money. HQ staff seemed quite committed and focused on preparing volunteers for their missions abroad. *Esprit de corps* was high.

The average volunteer age was twenty-eight, with a majority being women. Volunteers trained in country up to three months, usually staying with host families, where language and cultural skills were assimilated. Two years was the required tour, with another year possible. Because of rigorous training and history, the Peace Corps was considered the world's premier volunteer organization.

Under George W. Bush's administration, the Peace Corps enjoyed support from both political parties. Though begun by a Democrat, JFK, its headquarters building and fellowship were named after GOP Senator Coverdell. Its budget then was $330 million, a drop in the bucket compared to the USG's over trillion-dollar budget. US taxpayers got much bang for their buck.

Ambassador René from El Salvador affirmed, "The Peace Corps is the best of America. Our country appreciates the volunteers—especially the good they do for people in our interior."

So where did I misstep? I asked myself later. Was it speaking too much *español* with the recently appointed Hispanic director? Was it too much flamboyance in a culture focused on mission? Perhaps it was my Latino lunches, inviting people outside the Peace Corps to exchange ideas off the record. Yet in DC, is anything off the record if someone else overhears?

Enough of organizational intrigue! With my Deputy's assistance, I got to know IAP's staff and visiting country directors when they came through DC. At weekly senior staff meetings, I'd report key developments in the region—especially any incidents involving volunteers. We each carried Blackberry devices and were on call 24-7 if anything happened in our region.

As two of the largest programs in the Peace Corps resided in Central America, I flew first to Guatemala, past active volcanoes and verdant hills. Many of the 280 volunteers were in villages distant from the capital. They often had to think on their feet as situations popped up. A key ingredient was the volunteer's relationship with the village leader, who provided guidance and heads-up. Programs like preventative medicine and small business were in high demand, and the country team worked closely with local leaders to open doors and stay current.

Country director Charlie was supported by a UW friend and former chamber president, Mario, who visited the PC's training center in Antigua. It was fun seeing my friend after several years, who cautioned about traffickers trying to gain foothold. Unfortunately, violence in the country increased, and PC's program later wound down in this country of Mayan tradition.

My next visit was to Honduras, historically connected with the United Fruit Co., growing and exporting bananas to American markets. Known as "the Octopus" in Latin press, United Fruit's CEO was so stressed that he jumped out the window of the Pan Am Building when bribes to Honduras's president became known. This was the country backdrop where we had three hundred PCVs, one of whom I met at El Cantoral.

"So, Michael, tell me your story, as you seem a hero to these people on the hill," I said.

"I ran 5Ks in college—good training to run up and down Honduran hills," he affirmed.

"So is running part of your task as volunteer?" I inquired to this fit young man.

"My task is to help our community plant new produce besides traditional crops," he said. "So I often run down the hill to the highway to catch a ride to Tegucigalpa's market in the morning."

"I once lived on a hill in Rio, so I credit your energy to get their produce to market. Also, why did your community choose bok choy as its cash crop?"

"Our village leader and I visited the market thirty miles away, and found bok choy's prices higher than other produce. We talked it over with community farmers and planted last year. Now they reap the rewards, with higher family income," he said, excusing himself to run down the hill.

The village spoke highly of Michael, proudly showing their bok choy and long carrots to this visitor from Washington.

Back in DC, Bush II ramped up rhetoric and actions in the Middle East, while the Peace Corps kept low profile, sending volunteers abroad. I began monthly luncheons in local bistros inviting guests from the State Department, Partners of the Americas, and local think tanks, discussing issues of international development in Latin America. Friends from Heritage once joined us for lunch, but the director took issue, as this foundation had much power. He wanted control of all outreach in this political town.

So I pulled in my horns and refocused on our marriage plans. We were both restive by separation, so Vicki visited that fall. I showed off the other Washington, which she liked a lot. We looked for possible residence—especially in Arlington. We found a new apartment in Courthouse, with pedestrian walkways and cafés, including Sawatdee, our favorite Thai bistro. Access to the metro was a plus.

I hit the road again to escape DC's politics—this time to the Caribbean, where I helped dig ditches with RPCVs in Kingston. Unable to go to Jamaica's north shore, my letter to Herbert and his family had not received response. On to Haiti and the Dominican Republic I went, witnessing tougher circumstance since my last visit. I spoke with volunteers in the DR who appreciated RPCV John and Tom's foundations, supporting training and small business loans.

At Christmas, I returned to Seattle, missing the White House walkthrough for political appointees. I did receive a White House ornament, which I put in Vicki's stocking. We had a pre-Christmas dinner for our wedding party and set our date after Valentine's Day at St. Bridget's Catholic

Church. We went to midnight Mass and looked forward to our nuptial celebration.

Costa Rica's program invited me to its fortieth anniversary, visiting Limon, San José, and smaller villages, home of more than one hundred volunteers. Working in youth projects and teaching ESL, the volunteers liked this ecologically friendly country, many staying after tour. I met one RPCV who raised monarch butterflies and sent larvae to museums around the world. In Nicaragua, I gave kudos to PC outreach to rural villages and found a volunteer working with an Agros community. In Panama, it felt better this time without Noriega. I met volunteers in water projects, helping indigenous communities passed by Panama's real estate boom.

On return to DC, I spent little down time but was blessed by an early gift from Byron, who'd open our program in Mexico. He and his wife had a flat on Paris's Left Bank, offering it to Vicki and me as a honeymoon present—*merci beaucoup!*

In Seattle, our marriage countdown continued, and I said a prayer to keep me on track. On February 15, three hundred friends and family poured into St. Bridget's, wanting to see Vicki and me walk down the aisle. Catholic priests John and Harry, as well as UPC Pastor Earl officiated, making sure we'd be duly blessed. "You finally did it," said my longstanding friend Keith, maybe fearing me too set in my ways. Yet I gulped again, went out on the ledge, and gave my promise to Vicki to be faithful, in good times or bad. Brazilian friends from Tempero provided tasty hors d'oeuvres to guests waiting in line.

That night, we checked into a high-tech hotel in Woodinville without knobs and switches. We had hard times figuring out the showers or the lighting systems. Instead, we lit candles and found a CD, playing songs from *Raiders of the Lost Ark* over and over again.

In the morning, we flew over the pole to Paris and began our romantic honeymoon in Byron's flat in Saint-Germain-des-Pres. We savored long lunches at Le Procope and visited friends in several arrondissements. We met up with Eliane, who invited us to her favorite bistro at La Bastille and proved herself as diplomat par excellence. I made a silly mistake, though, by suggesting Chinese dinner in this city of fine cuisine. Vicki and I both got food poisoning big time and became intimate in a hurry, beating feet to the WC. Notwithstanding my choice of bistro, our honeymoon was grand, and Paris's weather was abiding. We still look at the photos along the Seine, across Pont Neuf, where we walked hand in hand.

At Charles De Gaulle, we embraced and bid *a bientot*, as Vicki flew to Seattle and yours truly to the other Washington. The work environment proved chillier as a PC volunteer went AWOL. I spent the weekend making calls to Paraguay and monitoring my Blackberry. Fortunately, she was found with her local boyfriend but putting us to fright as we searched 24-7.

Vicki arrived in April and put feminine touches in the stark apartment. We began attending Our Lady Queen of Peace in South Arlington, Virginia, with other RPCVs, often bringing up the gifts to the altar. Socially, we attended PC events and a few soirees but generally spent time together, getting to know one another.

In May, I had occasion to return to Brazil, touching base with the ambassador's staff and to Agencia Brasileira de Cooperação. ABC sent Brazilian technicians abroad to countries in need, with programs in Bolivia and Mozambique, overlapping with Peace Corps. I was hopeful the PC's director would abide communication, possibly joining forces with this emerging country overseas. The last RPCV's left Brazil under the Carter Administration, but nurtured hope for greater cooperation.

On return to DC, instead of plaudits, I received frowns. Though all diplomatic conversations were noncommittal, they were not part of the director's agenda. Thus, while I saw promise in opening doors to Brazil's ABC, he saw red. Our personalities had not clicked from day one, nor did they click post-Brazil.

Inside the Beltway, power ruled the roost. Unless a greater force from the president's office intervened, the secretary or director controlled the fate of political appointees like me. I had met President George W. Bush once in a reception line but did know his chief of staff, embroiled in the politics of Iraq. Despite my early hopes in the Peace Corps, it was not to be in DC. I left the second semester 2003, hoping not to fall off the edge.

In those circumstances, I withdrew to lick my wounds. Vicki was supportive but concerned. I continued to attend World Bank's Bible study over lunch on Wednesdays, appreciating friends like Alwyn, Joseph, and Samiha's prayers, to continue my journey.

That year, I founded, with Partners of the Americas, a new fund to promote literacy throughout the Americas to kids at risk. Partners, initiated under JFK, provided partnerships between North and South American counterparts, sponsoring exchanges in art, education, and small business. In our state of Washington, we partnered with Chile with lively engagements.

Family and friends helped fund the Pixote Literacy Fund, named after *Pixote*, or *little one* in Portuguese, featured in Hector Babenco's film on street kids in São Paulo. He permitted use of his film title as long as we assisted the lead actor's daughter in education. We did so and have provided grants for teachers, books, and literacy programs all over the Americas. Check us out at www.partners.net/pixote.

Later in the fall, I had dinner with my former Columbia professor and then president of the Inter-American Development Bank. Dr. Enrique mentioned the bank's initiative to help small businesses as well as improve remittance flows in *las Americas*. He connected me with the manager of its Multilateral Investment Fund, Don, who later hired me as senior advisor.

Don was especially passionate about remittances, trying to lower transfer expenses of dollar remittances to families in the Americas. The MIF and Inter-American Dialogue elevated remittances as a key development issue, as $50 billion was sent annually to families south of the border.

Don had worked on Capitol Hill and at the Treasury Department for Democratic administrations before joining MIF, but he was passionate about his work: "Steve, we need help in Brazil where you've spent many years. What do you suggest?"

"Though the bank is known in Brazil, it'd be politic to join forces with Brazilian institutes, like Fundação Getulio Vargas," I responded, sensing good vibes from my new boss.

"Do you think Brazilians would respond to a conference on remittances if Brazilian partners and speakers were involved?"

"I believe so, but Brazil's bureaucracy is extensive. I'd recommend visiting organizations in Brasilia as well as Brazil's ambassador and consuls general in the United States too," I affirmed.

"I understand that your former BankBoston colleague is now president of Brazil's central bank. Do you think he'd be willing to speak?"

"Let me visit him and see what he thinks," I replied and set off on my dream mission to my adopted country again.

The next months proved delightful, and friends at FGV and Brazil's central bank concurred. We held Brazil's first conference on remittances the following year at Rio's Hotel Meridien, with hundreds of attendees. My BKB colleague Henrique gave the opening address, which was carried by Brazil's media on evening TV. Recently, despite Brazil's recent turbulence, Henrique was tapped to serve as Finance Minister to bring his country back from the brink. At our conference, his speech mobilized new partners to enter the remittance flow business, lowering costs to Brazilian recipients—our ultimate goal.

As my one-year contract came to an end, I became restless in DC—now going into three years. Vicki still worked as a social worker in downtown DC and enjoyed her job, even if pay was slim. After some months with low income in pricey DC, we spoke about returning to the hometown. As I secured consulting work with a Seattle private equity group, we made plans for Vicki to stay in DC until I found a place to stay in my trendier hometown. I crossed the country again in my stalwart Saturn II and returned to DC in February 2005.

Vicki and I left the Beltway, traversing our country for our second honeymoon. No Blackberries joined us—or gruff chiefs of staff. Instead we did light battle with winter's forces across the Midwest. Our special moment was at Bear Lake, dividing Utah and Idaho. Under light snowfall, we viewed its turquoise waters under winter sun, breathing deeply its fresh air. No Beltway gridlock there! Instead an elk herd graced our horizon, as our compass pointed northwest.

CHAPTER 11

Issaquah (Mission Havana)

THE EMERALD CITY welcomed us with winter's bluster, rains blowing in from Puget Sound. Thanks to pledge brother Harley, we secured an apartment in Shoreline above Richmond Beach. I took walks along its shore, waving to Amtrak passengers heading to Vancouver, BC. In mist or rain, I'd jog back with my hoodie tight, not minding Seattle's weather—I was back on home turf.

Vicki returned to Valley Medical Center, which welcomed her as social worker. She'd commute up and down I-5 in mega-traffic, returning bedraggled at night. We'd unwind over sauvignon blanc, with yours truly as thoughtful listener—but not to opine. Afterward, I'd prepare dinner with pleasure, chopping up vegetables with ginger or garlic, thankful they couldn't talk back.

Later, we looked for residence closer to her work—at a time of real estate frenzy. We got outbid on a Hawthorne Hills home by a hundred grand, so retreated across Lake Washington. We found a three-bedroom home, closed the deal, and moved in that spring with cherry blossoms giving welcome. We enjoyed proximity to Issaquah's charming downtown and visited galleries on first Friday's art walk. In this town meaning "sound of birds" or "little stream" in indigenous tongue, we've made our home.

Professionally, I rejoined consulting consortium, Pacific Northwest Advisors, marketing small businesses expanding south of the border. My clients included software firms seeking licensees—especially in Brazil. At Seattle U, I returned to part-time teaching. At the University of Washington, I connected with Foster Business School students, recruiting some as interns for Latin America.

Socially, fellow *latinistas* founded Latino Dining, breaking bread monthly at family bistros around Puget Sound. Founding members Lyle, John, Jean, and Paula became mainstay diners over ten years, and we include some favorites below:

- Tempero do Brasil in Seattle's University District with Graça's tasty Bahian dishes
- El Quetzal on Beacon Hill for Juan's fine Mexican cuisine near El Centro de la Raza
- Café con Leche, serving savory Cuban meals south of Starbucks headquarters
- Vuelve a la Vida (Return to Life) for delicious seafood ceviche, *a la* Sr. Douglas

As AIESEC's first intern to Brazil, I joined its board of advisors on UW's campus, reconnecting with students and promoting international exchange. AIESEC has chapters in more than one hundred countries, offering student internships, including in Latin America. Campus involvement proves thrilling as students keep this alumnus on his toes with questions that require thoughtful response.

Our household in Issaquah grew under Vicki's aegis, adding a tabby mother and her rambunctious son, running up and down our stairs and screen door *a la* Garfield in cartoons. Yet the apple of her eye was Mariah, her Lhasa Apso, approaching fifteen years. Gardening continued to be her favorite pastime, her green thumb working wonders at Issaquah's public garden—especially, zucchini.

Little by little, I acclimated to sharing our household together, becoming more flexible despite different habits. Vicki was still a night person, as I once was, but hubby became early to bed and early to rise.

During this writing experience, I've gone AWOL, hiding in remote places or Internet cafés. I'll break out for date night, enjoying popular bistros like the Flat Iron Grill in Gilman Village, where we dine on tapas beneath the willows.

We also went church shopping on the eastside, visiting lively parishes like St. Louise or St. Madeleine Sophie. We settled on St. Joseph's of Issaquah, within walking distance from our home and joined its Bible study, thanks to its stalwart leader, Tom. We've appreciated sharing observations and doubts in small groups with stimulating discussion of the Word. I've found such fellowship meaningful in my daily walk of faith, despite an increasingly secular world. I've enjoyed making *guacamole a la Esteban* for Tom's summertime BBQ or Christmas potluck at parishioners Dino and Terry's nice home. It goes fast, so come early!

By now, maybe some readers have tuned down their attention, as my life appears more subdued. My adventures have not been as edgy of late, like facing the Pacific typhoon or bobbing on a shrimp boat to islands unknown. When I fly to South America on business, how can it compare to hitchhiking from George Washington Bridge to the Yucatán on a wing and a prayer? Still, I'll share different experiences, which may liven the pot at this point of my journey.

Reconnecting with the UW, I occasionally visited my chapter of Phi Kappa Psi. I recalled past ties, including brothers' invite to Portales decades ago, providing *destination*, as I exited HBS, my tail between my legs. Cross-country, I visited other chapters, interacting with fellow brothers, whose fellowship helped heal my broken dreams.

From Vietnam, I'd written for the fraternity's *Shield*, reaching out to veterans in an unpopular war. Arriving at Columbia to complete my MBA, Phi Psi's nominal chapter secured me a closet as my abode. I've felt gratitude toward our noble fraternity, cherishing longstanding friendships with pledge brothers, like Harley and Keith.

So when, out of the blue, I was invited to dinner at the chapter house, I said yes. Its outgoing president Sean was friendly, inviting me and incoming Bryce to the library to chat. In my day, that room was used to hot-box, incoming students they wanted to pledge. That evening, I sensed something was up, as my conversation with both presidents went like this:

"Steve, we appreciate your stopping by now and again. The brothers get a lot from alumni speakers you invite. We hope you'll bring more!" Sean began.

I nodded my head, saying, "Happy to do so," wondering where he was going with this.

"You see," continued Bryce, "we need more alumni like you to connect with undergrads. Would you like to get more involved at chapter?"

"Sure, Bryce. What do you both have in mind?"

Then Bryce dropped the question: "Would you become our chapter advisor?" Sean smiled with enthusiasm.

Wow, I thought—I wasn't expecting that, so I inquired, "What happened to Craig? He's been doing a good job."

"He and his wife are expecting," Sean said. "He won't have much time. He'll be raising his family instead."

So I took a deep breath and said, "Sure, guys—with pleasure."

Little did I know, that such simple affirmation, made five years ago, would have profound impact on me.

Sharing more fully, I confess that after leaving Hong Kong while in the navy, I began receiving letters from Nancy, sent to USS *Goldsborough*. She confirmed being pregnant, believing it mine. I was doubtful, so let it slide. Several years later, a friend visited her home in Fanling, confirming a young Eurasian boy of uncertain lineage.

Enjoying my life out and about in Rio, I'd avoided personal engagements or responsibilities at that time. Besides, the boy could have been of any GI, or so I rationalized. When another friend visited in the late eighties, neighbors said that she'd left with another, and her son had joined the merchant marine.

So when I encountered Beto in Rio, his words touched deeply within, pushing me beyond my comfort zone to reach out to street kids.

My actions to help out youth likely reflect my hidden grief, certainly regret, and maybe guilt. In the middle of night, I've asked myself where goes this person of Eurasian descent? Or Beto in Brazil—where does he rest his head? Inside, both "kids" travelled with me in this journey called life, gnawing my spirit, leaving a hole in my heart.

Thus, that offer conferred after chapter dinner had greater significance beyond first imagined. Our extended fraternal family has lent me vibrancy and purpose. I pray my engagement with students has served them well, as they consider future courses while life speeds by. I give it my all.

So there it is—my secret is out. I continue onward, seeking significance in the lives of others, my days still numbered. With Vicki in Issaquah, I've reached equilibrium while pushing the envelope at a slower pace.

Notwithstanding GOP skepticism about Castro's regime, I've often believed engagement a more constructive approach. When the Obama administration announced intention to open dialogue with Raul, my ears perked up. Speaking with visitors, they painted a country of contrasts. I figured it was time to find out as senior advisor for Latin America.

When I spoke with José Antonio in Mexico City, he affirmed association with University of Havana as visiting professor. He thought such return would prove timely to discern how Raul's opening played on the street. With entrée to UH's dean of business, he set up appointments, his university maintaining open relations.

Flying to Havana on US flights or tours proved pricey. I checked with cousin Rick in La Paz, Baja California Sur, who found Mexican options at half the price. BKB alumni chair asked if I'd locate Banco de Boston's building where Uncle Frank once reigned supreme. I concurred and agreed to investigate Cuba's goatskin market for another BKB alum, whose tannery sought more hides.

In Seattle, I wrote letters to high profile impresarios, without response, reinventing my role as "emissary" for select organizations. Seattle U's business dean sent a finance textbook and its librarian another to counterparts at UH. Seattle International Film Festival bid me deliver invitations to filmmakers at Cuba's prestigious TV and Film School. Seattle's archdiocese connected me with Padre Juan in DC, providing entrée to Catholics in Havana.

We arrived in Havana in tropical heat. At immigration, they asked if I'd like my passport stamped. I declined, as diplomatic relations weren't yet in place. Our assigned transport dropped us at Hotel Victoria in Vedado, a prime tourist neighborhood. The front desk vaguely confirmed our reservation in its overbooked hotel, our bags taken by a middle-aged bellboy seeking dollar bills.

We walked to Hotel Nacional, scene of *The Godfather II*, dramatizing Castro's coming to power. After a while, we flagged a waiter, eventually savoring mojitos and admiring Caribbean waters of the Pearl of the Antilles. The hotel's senior doorman knew of ole Banco de Boston and gave directions to its building in Old Havana.

José Antonio led us to Universidad de Habana's campus, remarking at its replica of Columbia University's famous statue, *Alma Mater*. Like the Cuban capitol building, a replica of our own in DC, I couldn't help noticing US influence after fifty-five years. Especially colorful were vintage fifties automobiles chugging up El Malecón or navigating Old Havana's narrow streets.

The dean and vice dean welcomed José Antonio in open arms and affirmed UH's expanding curriculum in small business and tourism. I transmitted SU's book gifts and letters from its dean, librarian, and English professor, hoping to stimulate educational exchange. In between the lines, I understood that the state university's rector was a party member. Thus, deans, professors, and students were circumspect in commenting on campus about *el Comandante*, whose photos hung everywhere.

We invited the deans to lunch at a local *paladar*, a privately run restaurant offering better cuisine. The word *paladar* came from a Brazilian soap opera playing on Cuban TV, showing chic Rio bistros and gorgeous *mulatas*. That year, greater Havana counted a thousand of such bistros, often finding supplies in parallel markets. State food stores proved unreliable to many restaurateurs.

On Saturday morning, we went to Old Havana and were approached by a young couple: "*Buenos dias, señores*. Do you know who we are?"

"We're staying at Hotel Victoria," said José Antonio. "Do you work there?"

"We cook your breakfast but have a small request to make," the young sous chef replied. I nodded my head, and she continued, "Please come with us to a cigar parlor and buy some *habanos*. If you do, we'll gain a meal ticket, which will help us get by."

How could we say no? So we followed them upstairs to a private room selling *Montecristos* and *Cohiba* at $120 a box. Unfortunately, I only had twenty dollars, enough for four cigars but not for a meal ticket. The sous chefs were sad, as were we, but she left with three Cuban Units of Currency, with Che's image on the CUC's bill.

José Antonio returned home, and I sought Señor José, administrator for Havana's archdiocese. He left a planning session for Pope Francis's visit to briefly meet up. He asked about the Knights of Columbus's possible support for Catholic priests and for our prayers for Cuban churches. He accepted my gift of Washington State's Aplets & Colets, eating a couple while I bid him *adios*. He also provided entrée to the new rector of the Catholic *Centro Cultural*.

Sunday, I walked two miles to Old Havana to attend Mass, passing teens on the stairs. One of them, named Johnny, asked, "*Gringo, que pasa?*"

"Not much—I'm getting to know your beautiful city," I replied, smiling at his group of eight.

"Beautiful, nothing! We can't find work nor enough to eat! Why don't you put me in your backpack and take me home to America?" he asked.

"Do you want to go to Mass, Johnny? I'm heading to the Cathedral now." I inquired, looking for something to say.

"Gracias, no. The church and me—we don't mix much. But maybe some CUCs, if you have some on you?" I gave him a three CUC bill featuring Che and a Seattle postcard. I took photos of him and his extended family on the streets of Havana. I've sent him a copy.

After the ten-thirty Mass, I met Fr. Yosvany, setting another date to meet. I wandered the streets of Old Havana, past Hemingway's haunts and the former edifice of Banco de Boston. A couple of brothers took me back in their "new" Packard convertible, financed by cousins in Miami.

"You see, Esteban," they said, "Cuba has the world's best mechanics. To keep American cars running, we use Czech valves and Russian spark plugs. The tires are from China, but they wear out fast. We still get around after all these years."

The next day, I made another rookie mistake at breakfast, eating sardines on the buffet. Two hours later, I was running back and forth to the bathroom, loading myself with Lomotil. The brothers drove me to Old Havana, saying, "You don't look well, Esteban," dropping me off at the cultural center. There, I lost round one on the archbishop's garden, round two in the foot basin used by country priests, and round three in the toilet, looking a whiter shade of pale.

The rector sent for pills to counter food poisoning but found none at two pharmacies, offering tea instead. Fr. Yosvany said, "Yes, we have material poverty in Cuba, but spiritual poverty is greater after fifty-some years. Pray for us here." Under Raul's opening five years previously, local churches were asked to provide social services, receiving permission for more public worship. Attendance seemed up in Havana and the countryside, especially in new home churches, which were growing apace.

The center offered courses in humanities and small business for budding entrepreneurs, like the taxicab brothers, private *paladar* chefs, and cigar-shop owners. Cuba's people seemed enterprising and hardworking, and they would thrive if the system opened up. I bid, "*Hasta la vista*," to the Cubans I'd interviewed, keeping in touch despite precarious e-mail. I also vowed to never again eat sardines in Havana or other places where brown outs occur. "*Atención*," they'd say. "Take care."

I returned to the Emerald City with gusto, giving presentations to Seattle's business and university communities. A couple articles published in the *Puget Sound Business Journal* and at Seattle's Trade Development Alliance sparked interest to reengage with Cuba. At Pacific Northwest Advisors, we formed "Team Cuba" with Frank Carlos in Miami and Reynier in Havana, providing consulting and scarce accommodations amid Cuba's current land rush.

Enough of advertisements, as I ply the Cuba trade. At Casa Murphy, our life continues in lower key—a live-and-let-live attitude *entre nous*. We enjoy our community near Lake Sammamish and often picnic in the park. We still fight to keep our trees, while developers push up the sides of our hills, protesting with other citizens at Mayor Fred's coffee hours.

Phi Psi students just returned from the Big Apple, enthused by our fraternity's grand arch council, where UW alumnus Jim was elected as national president. For football aficionados, we look forward to positive seasons by both Coaches Pete, one with UW Huskies and the other with the Seahawks, XLVIII Super Bowl Champion—check us out.

For those visiting Seattle toward the end of every month, please join our "Mini Tigers" investor luncheon over paella and Don Ramon grenache. All conversations are off the record, and themes vary from month to month. Our fellowship has been ongoing for ten years, cofounded by Dr. Carl, a longstanding friend and UW classmate, retired doctor, and investor par excellence.

In our small community in the Cascade foothills, you may appreciate our evergreens, lakes, and living space not far from Seattle. If you come in early October, view wild salmon swimming upstream through Issaquah's creek.

On The Edge

When our town celebrates Salmon Days, search near the bandstand for our Knights' booth. I'll likely be serving churros, chocolate, or limeade. Come visit, and let's chat. Who knows? We may put our heads together and come up with another cause célèbre for the year ahead.

Be welcome.

CHAPTER 12

What's Next?

ONCE MORE, I climbed those long steps, reached the top, and looked over the edge. How many times had I done so as a younger man? I let a couple kids pass by so they could plunge first, while I grabbed extra breath. I jumped off, holding my nose, landing askew. I went down—probably deeper with more weight—climbing to the surface. My nose came up bloody from scratching it when I hit. My skin and body were more fragile than when I jumped fifty years ago.

Still, I continue swimming in open bodies of water, starting my season late April, usually lasting through October. My wife fears that I may suffer a heart attack when my body hits spring's cool waters. My response has been, "What a way to go—doing what I love!"

Throughout this journey, I've sought my raison d'etre in life. Despite personal zigzags, some conclusions have bubbled to the surface, which I share without pontification. Indeed, how could I possibly do so, after the life I've led? Below are some ideas, concluding this current chapter of odyssey.

"Who am I? Who are you?" At Phi Kappa Psi's American Leadership Academy, held during spring break, speakers Jerry and Paul asked students to pick ten attributes to define themselves as individuals. Each student wrote down ten, such as integrity, love, faith, family, honor and so on. Then, the facilitator asked us to cut the list in half and then again to three, asking each person what characteristics defined one's unique being. What

would yours be? My latest rendering included "friendship, perseverance, and faith."

The Purpose Driven Life is the book written by Rick Warren, asking, "What on earth am I here for?" It posits that each of us has eternal purpose beyond vagaries of cultural fads. President Obama thought highly of Rick's theme, asking him to deliver the inaugural invocation.

In my own case, I've asked why, as a young student in a blue-collar town, I felt drawn to people south of the border? Was it our Spanish teacher from Chihuahua State, wearing his sombrero, singing *norteñas* and making Spanish fun? Was it my Ecuadorian girlfriend and her lively salsa at Seattle World's Fair? Or was there an invisible hand behind the scenes with a longer game plan?

During my glamor years in Rio, feeling on top of the world, I wondered if there wasn't something more out there—was that all there was? Trying to keep God in a box, to not upset my lifestyle, I had a gnawing feeling that I'd have to open it up someday. Then my ah-ha moment in Miami, arrived, and life changed.

Over espresso with intern Zach in the atrium of UW's PACCAR Hall, we spoke about these themes.

"How do you know what your purpose in life is?" inquired this student, getting ready to earn his MBA.

"It takes a while, amigo. A priest once told me to pay attention to the little things of life. There may be signs that occur that aren't obvious at the time," I suggested.

"It's not easy, you know. I get caught up in life's pressures," he explained.

"True. It's important to take time to reflect, like we're doing now over *cafecito*."

"So what's your purpose, Steve, after all these years?"

"To build bridges with all peoples of the Americas," I affirmed. "You'll find yours, Zach, if you keep asking the question. Stay tuned, amigo. You'll get a sense of what it is."

* * *

"*Carpe Diem*," since written by the Roman poet Horace, has become a popular mantra to "seize the day." Horace's words still resonate—especially as I begin each day. I start, bowing my head on the prayer mat, which my brother brought from Oman. First, I give thanks to the Lord for another day on earth. I ask guidance for my day ahead. I pray for friends in need. That's how I begin my day, usually rising at dawn. My morning conversation with God has become a daily ritual, grounding me for what comes next. I'll also do sit-ups, one for each year, sometimes counting off in French, even Arabic, lest I forget.

Being a morning person, I may serve Vicki breakfast in bed, or if she has a late workday, I'll call her after 8:00 a.m. Let's hope I don't forget. During my outdoor season, I'll swim in three bodies of water; in winter, it's more boring, dividing time between pools in Issaquah and North Bend. Over macchiato in quaint cafés, I'll e-mail friends and family or Skype a client somewhere abroad. I'll still look forward to lunch with friends. If solo, I'll frequent bistros along Front Street.

If no deadline is weighing down, I'll usually return home on our hill, climb upstairs, and take a nap. I'll look forward to preparing dinner when Vicki returns, maybe a BBQ on the deck beneath our cedars. On Wednesday evenings, I may walk down the community path, enshrouded by trees, and cross the block in time for St. Joe's Bible fellowship. On the way back—especially during winter nights—I've been known to say Psalm 23, entering the dark woods where bear and coyote roam.

Variety is the spice of life. By now, some readers may be rolling their eyes, thinking, *Is that all I get in this last chapter?* Not quite yet. Even though routine's important, I might still venture back to the edge. Hopefully now, I'll use more wisdom but still act out, as in Cuba, on paths less travelled. While serving as a bridge between peoples of the Americas, I must always be ready to act. Just letting life go by doesn't cut it for me.

While travel isn't as fun as it used to be, visiting another place, people, and culture is always thrilling to me. Even in quieter Issaquah, I can always opt for conversation with another human being, and who knows what such encounter might bring?

On The Edge

People over places. My last Sunday morning in New York, after the fraternity's council, I had to choose where to spend scarce time before the airport—visit the 9/11 memorial or go to a parish, possibly meeting people at Mass. I chose the latter and attended St. Patrick's on Fifth Avenue, offering parishioners the sign of peace. Afterward, I wandered through Rockefeller Center, finding the French bakery, Bouchon. Its doors would open at 9:00 a.m., so I sat outside, writing this memoir's chapter 10. Another man my age, having walked his daily ten miles, came by, striking up conversation.

He was still working on Wall Street, though times weren't booming in his IPO niche—fewer firms were going public in 2016. We kibitzed on issues, ranging from finance, sports, and even religion. Over croissant and cappuccino, we had a delightful give-and-take before heading our separate ways. I make this decision every time I visit a new city. I seek out people over places, with scarce time allotted. Nevertheless, I do want to visit Ground Zero, especially to honor its dead.

Fellowship, yes, begins at home. But it's important to reach beyond. I've spoken of our Bible study, Latino Dining, and "Mini Tiger" luncheons, finding such engagements stimulating—might you, perhaps, in a different setting? While breaking bread with mere acquaintances, over the years, we've now become friends. Sometimes we linger after such encounters, not wanting to leave.

As readers of books, have you considered joining a book club? Thanks to Peter, Vince, and Skip's invite, I've felt blessed to attend their Magnolia group, reviewing five books a year. Though we're unlikely to agree on politics, we enjoy our tête-à-tête and even summer picnics.

At UW's Phi Kappa Psi, annual turnover continues as students come and go, with more graduations on the horizon. Staying connected with young alums can be fun, following their careers and offering insights if asked. Who knows—we might be able to exchange referrals and continue our friendship over the years.

I attend quarterly luncheons at Seattle's yacht club, catching up with alumni in different stages of life. Come fall, I plan to attend UW football with Keith and hit homecoming—go Dawgs! As years run on, I'll join more reunions, closely checking those nametags. I look forward to celebrating UW's fiftieth for the Class of 1966—it was a very good year!

How should I measure success? If I measure success by worldly standards, many suggestions come via reality TV. Wealth, glamor, prestige—I sought them all before March 1995 but didn't find solace in their pursuit. Rick Warren's measurement by a higher standard may offer alternatives to current mores.

My dad and I spoke briefly about being significant in life. He wisely advised that his impact on the lives of others would only become apparent on his demise: How many people would honor him? Judging by the overflowing attendance at his memorial, my father was a resounding success.

On the Edge. In reviewing this memoir and reliving adventures, I wonder if I'd do it again. But it's done, and I'm going to make the best of it. For younger persons in love with lifestyle or transient things, you may wish to take pause. If you'd like to leave your mark on humanity, consider doing so while you have time, for who knows the morrow?

While other forces may cause us to stumble, let us shake off the dust, rising again and preparing for life's next battle. Push the envelope, yes, in good faith and intentions. Take time to reflect. But act. Indeed, *act*, even if it brings you closer to the edge.

As I stretch myself toward new situations—even uncomfortable ones— I'll give it my best shot. I'll say my daily prayers, keeping eyes and ears open. To stand pat is death. So I'll keep on keeping on, alert to what's next just around the corner.

Acknowledgments

A FRIEND IN DC reminded that this memoir should be real and not invented, sharing fears and concerns—without too many details. I thank Bill for his suggestion and have endeavored to do so—I hope I've met your expectations. Besides my memory, which my wife deems "selective" over time, I thank all the friends and family who've jogged recollection of shared experiences, including from these organizations: Harvard Business School, Phi Kappa Psi Fraternity, the US Navy, Columbia Business School, AIESEC, BankBoston (BKB), Paramount Pictures, Universal Studios, the Motion Picture Association, the US Information Agency (the State Department), the Peace Corps, the Inter-American Development Bank, the University of Washington, Seattle University, *Fundação Getulio Vargas*, Partners of the Americas, Pacific Northwest Advisors, and the Catholic church.

In addition to my loving parents, I give special thanks to that anonymous priest who heard me out that lonely winter night.

I thank the generous Caseys of Boston and families in Rio, São Paulo, Oaxaca, Paris, Cuzco, Namitembo, Robin's Bay, Santiago, and around the world for their friendship as these years fly by. *Gracias*, fellow *latinistas*—especially Jeb—for moral support as I ran the gauntlet inside DC's Beltway.

Thank you, students of Miami Jackson High School, who encouraged my spiritual odyssey in your lively hometown, including Richard's renderings for my cover design.

I so appreciate our cadre from Puget Sound, whom I highlight below:

- Spencer Berry, UW student and cover designer—*gracias*—you have a great future ahead.
- Rick Edelman, photographer par excellence—thanks for putting together the great collage.
- Dennis Gibbs, author and fund manager—thank you for your inspiration and keen insights.

To friends Bill, Lucja, Carl, Christopher, Connie, Riley, Marcos, Steve, James, John, Nicky, Joe, Sergio, Silvia, Ari, Alberto, Frank, Fr. Todd, Tom, Don, and my sister, Pamela—I'm grateful for your critiques and hope you find this final version engaging. Thank you Jonathan, Georges, Roberto, Barbara, Janice, Julianne, and Zach for brainstorming on the memoir's title and cover design—your input is valuable, so what do you think? Thanks to Spencer L. for putting this book on Facebook and Andy on Linked In, notwithstanding its low tech author. Thank you editors Abigail and Jon for your TLC and Erinn for her help in navigating CreateSpace.

And thank you, Vicki, for putting up with a reclusive hubby these past months. I promise to become more sociable once *On the Edge: An Odyssey* goes to print and to journey with you to your favorite park in Colorado, *si Dios quiere.*

Thank you, Ron, for recommending my "book coach," Bruce, of Orange, California, who has cheered me while providing tough love.

I recognize too members of UW's class reunion committee—especially Nicky and Al—for their leadership among our sixties generation. Encouragement by classmates to "write it down" was material to start my memoir this year and to finish it in time for our fiftieth reunion.

As part of the University of Washington's fiftieth reunion committee, I share these poignant and exhilarating experiences with recent graduates. I toast those students who've received our UW Class of 1966 scholarships in the past and to you winners in the future.

Carpe diem!